More Praise for *7 Days to Change Your Life*

"In *7 Days to Change Your Life*, Pastor Josh Moody artistically takes the beauty of the biblical text to paint a vibrant picture of Christian discipleship. The colors of the gospel and Christ's atoning work on the cross are brilliantly portrayed in such soul-rocking, life-changing themes as hope, humility, and truth. Wonderfully accessible and culturally relatable, the book is destined to draw believers young and old to a fuller and ever-flourishing relationship with the King of Kings. A must read!"

—HAROLD B. SMITH, President and CEO, *Christianity Today*

"Readers of this work will join me in offering gratitude to Josh Moody for writing this insightful, encouraging, and challenging work. In *7 Days to Change Your Life*, Moody invites us to new commitments and fresh understandings of what it means to follow Christ. Rather than presenting readers with a how-to model of discipleship, we are presented with a beautiful tapestry shaped by the themes of hope, life, truth, freedom, humility, greatness, and glory. I am confident that readers will find real guidance and genuine enablement in the pages of this thoughtful and readable volume. It is joy for me to commend this new work."

—DAVID S. DOCKERY, President, Trinity Evangelical Divinity School

"When Josh Moody found himself in need of personal revitalization having spent years helping others with similar needs and aspirations he was disappointed that he could not find a book that said what he and those to whom he ministered thought they needed to hear. So rather than curse the darkness he decided to light a candle—behold the candle now shines in the shape of *7 Days to Change Your Life*. In this book, Josh hits the nail on the head when he talks about people who are tired or bored or disappointed with the way their lives are working out and would love the start again. At the risk of sounding simplistic he tells us that the way to start again or to experience a revitalization is to change your mind about what you've been doing and rethink where you're wanting to go. But here's the point—this change of mind is linked to Jesus, and the revitalized life is called 'Following Jesus.' Th̶ involves knowing what He said and doi̶ ̶ emulating it (with human limitations!);

and heeding them; embracing His promises and claiming them. These principles are spelled out to be digested in a week—you have the rest of your life for them to be implemented."

—STUART BRISCOE, speaker, author, broadcaster on *Telling the Truth*

"The biggest need in the church today is for more disciples. Not hipper preachers or dazzling worship or even stunning sanctuaries. The biggest need is for more believers to follow after Jesus and become authentic disciples. Josh Moody has provided a great service to the church in that pursuit with *7 Days to Change Your Life*. Absorb its contents, meditate on its message, and learn exactly how to leave your past behind and experience a future walk that is life-changing."

—J. PAUL NYQUIST, President, Moody Bible Institute, Chicago, IL

"From mature Christians in need of a spiritual tune-up to new Christians trying to figure out the implications of their newfound faith, even to thoughtful non-Christians looking to discover what real Christianity is all about, this readable book could be just what the doctor ordered. Its relentless focus on what it means to follow Jesus is the right prescription for all such readers. In fact, seven days with this book will be life-changing for any and all who are willing to embrace its godly counsel."

—DUANE LITFIN, President Emeritus of Wheaton College

"In *7 Days to Change Your Life*, Josh Moody makes a bold promise of life change . . . and delivers it. Josh invites us to follow Jesus as the disciples he has called us to be. In this accessible volume, you'll be able to jump in quickly but still come out changed."

—ED STETZER, Billy Graham Distinguished Chair, Wheaton College

"Pastor Josh Moody, serving in a vibrant evangelical church centered in a college setting, understands fully that in the life of a local, biblical fellowship both evangelism and discipleship ministries are two wings on the same plane. Without either focus, the airplane can't fly. In this creative book, Moody presents the challenge of authentic discipleship—knowing that when an individual comes to Christ (evangelism), the necessary next step is to grow like Him and exhibit the graces and life attributes that come only in 'knowing Christ and the power of His resurrection.' This rich, seven-day curriculum brings to sharp focus and creative application that transformational discipleship so necessary for both the individual believer and the corporate church body."

—DAVID BRUCE, executive assistant to Billy Graham, Billy Graham Evangelistic Association

"Are you weary in your walk with the Lord? Has it become routine, mundane, joyless? In this book, you will find a challenge to start again—a 7-day plan that is guaranteed to renew, refresh, and redirect your relationship with the Savior. If you are ready to respond when Jesus says, 'Follow Me,' then open the pages of this book and get ready for the journey of a lifetime!"

—JANET PARSHALL, nationally syndicated talk show host

"Josh Moody creatively and compellingly makes the case that following Christ is the heart of discipleship. From biblical texts and themes, and from his own experience, he guides us to new depths of understanding and faithful motivation as followers of Jesus in everyday life."

—DENNIS P. HOLLINGER, Ph.D., President & Colman M. Mockler Distinguished Professor of Christian Ethics, Gordon Conwell Theological Seminary

"As Christians, we too often separate our activities—such as sharing the gospel, doing justice, and caring for others from our inner spiritual journey. By focusing on virtues such as hope, humility, and truth, Josh Moody bridges this gap. He encourages us to be contemplative activists, having both deep roots and wide branches."

—ALEC HILL, President Emeritus, InterVarsity Christian Fellowship

"Josh Moody is a biblical scholar and a pastor who loves the people he serves. In his book, he uses the structure of a 7-day week to provide an insightful and thoughtful understanding of our role as disciples of Christ. In so doing, he reminds us of the importance of knowing the Jesus we serve, understanding the depth of His love for us, and experiencing the reality of having a relationship with Him for now and eternity. When the week is over, the reader will have a new and refreshed understanding of their Lord and Savior."

—C. WILLIAM POLLARD, Chairman, Fairwyn Investment Company

"Taking his point of departure from Jesus' seven 'Follow me!' statements in Matthew's Gospel, Josh Moody beckons you to follow him on a

7-day journey to revitalize your life—a time to reflect, refocus, and be refreshed spiritually. Highly recommended!"
—ANDREAS KÖSTENBERGER, author of *Excellence*, founder of Biblical Foundations (www.biblicalfoundations.org), and ministry council member of The God-Centered Life

"Pastor Josh Moody creatively weaves together themes from several key New Testament texts to exhort and encourage Christians to pursue a God-honoring, Christ-exalting lifestyle."
—DOUGLAS J. MOO, Wessner Chair of Biblical Studies, Wheaton College; chair, Committee on Bible Translation

"We forget so easily who we are as Christians and what we are called to do. Moody reminds us afresh what it means to be a follower of Jesus. In a profound and yet simple way, we are addressed anew by Jesus Christ himself as Moody unpacks the call to discipleship."
—THOMAS R. SCHREINER, James Buchanan Harrison Professor of New Testament Interpretation, Associate Dean, The Southern Baptist Theological Seminary

"I love the idea of a seven-day personal revival and recommitment of what it means to truly follow Jesus! Josh Moody is going against the tide of endless technology and communication by challenging us to turn off our phones and TVs at home and to ponder God's Word, grow in grace and truth, and walk in the footsteps of our Savior."
—TREVIN WAX, Bible and Reference Publisher for LifeWay Christian Resources, author of *This Is Our Time*, *Gospel-Centered Teaching*, and *Counterfeit Gospels*

"Josh Moody offers the church a great gift in this engaging and timely call to radical Christian discipleship. Filled with biblical insight and pastoral wisdom, *7 Days to Change Your Life* provides a clear and Christ-centered road map to the abundant life. If we desire to follow Jesus in the midst of our current cultural pressures, we cannot afford to ignore his appeal."
—DAVID SETRAN, Price-Lebar Chair of Christian Formation and Ministry, Wheaton College

"Josh Moody provides a unique look at what it means to follow Jesus, using thoughtful illustrations from a wide historical and cultural spectrum. In *7 Days to Change Your Life*, new believers will acquire a deeper understanding of true discipleship, and seasoned saints will find fresh zeal to persevere."

—LYDIA BROWNBACK, author, *Finding God in My Loneliness* and *A Woman's Wisdom*

"The problem with some tools offering help to the weary and puzzled Christian is that they tend to be patchy and selective. They seem to solve an issue but they eventually raise another one. Not so with Josh Moody's book. Instead of suggesting simplistic how-to solutions, he presents a reorientation of one's own Christian walk in terms of biblical discipleship. A mine of biblical wisdom interwoven with pastoral experience and theological insightfulness to refocus our journey on a God-centered life."

—LEONARDO DE CHIRICO, pastor and theologian, Rome (Italy), director of the Reformanda Initiative

"The rediscovery of Scripture-based thoughtful Christianity in the USA has been one of the most exciting things to happen to Evangelicalism in a long time. This wonderful Bible-centered book is a fabulous example of how to follow Jesus as God's Word shows us, showing how its clear teaching transforms our lives in a profoundly practical and entirely life-changing way. This book is how discipleship ought to be, the true joys of Christian living, and I am thrilled to commend and endorse it as enthusiastically as possible."

—CHRISTOPHER CATHERWOOD, historian, writer, and author of *Martyn Lloyd-Jones: His Life and Relevance for the 21st Century*

"*7 Days to Change Your Life* by Josh Moody is a rich devotional book written by a theologian pastor who is gospel centered, culturally savvy, and discipleship driven. This devotional book is not a surface, light read for the casual fan of Jesus, but a thorough exposition of the call to follow Jesus. Read this book and be informed, enriched, and transformed."

—JIM TOMBERLIN, author, founder of MultiSite Solutions

"Dr. Josh Moody provides a much-needed devotional guide in this day and age for a world which desperately craves and needs spiritual guidance but may not know it. Beautifully written like a parable, this helpful book, structured around the number 7 (the 7 days of Creation,

Jesus's 7 signs, his 7 'follow me' and 'I Am' statements, the 7 Churches of Revelation) refocuses the attention on what is most important."
—ALLEN YEH, Associate Professor of Intercultural Studies & Missiology, Biola

"There is a lot of confusion in the evangelical church about what it truly means to follow Jesus. Many Christians talk about the call to discipleship, but in the midst of our busy lives, many of us fail to consider what the Bible says about this call. So turn away from distractions and let Josh Moody help you see anew what John's Gospel and Revelation teach us about this simple call and lifelong challenge. You will benefit tremendously from this renewed vision of what it means to be a disciple of Jesus."
—CHRIS BRUNO, author, *The Whole Message of the Bible in 16 Words* and *The Whole Story of the Bible in 16 Verses*

"Josh Moody is a pastor, a scholar, and, above all, one who wants to love and follow Jesus Christ. With this book, he guides us on a journey that stirs, refreshes, and challenges. I believe you will find this book to be thoughtful, encouraging, insightful, and penetrating. No matter where you are on the path of knowing Jesus Christ, this will be a beneficial tool."
—CURTIS COOK, pastor of Hope Fellowship Church, Cambridge, MA

"After reading the first chapter, I found myself preparing for 7 days at the spiritual health spa where I'd be pampered and allowed to put my feet up. I couldn't have been more wrong! Josh's book shows us that restoration is found in the following of Jesus, which includes death to self but eventually results in an abundance of deep joy and life-giving freedom. Thank you for writing a book that seeks to challenge us and restores us to the Lord and Giver of Life."
—ROBERT KRUMREY, lead pastor of MERCYhouse in Amherst, MA

7 DAYS

TO CHANGE YOUR LIFE

FIND FOCUS THROUGH INTENTIONAL LIVING

JOSH MOODY

ABINGDON PRESS
NASHVILLE

7 DAYS TO CHANGE YOUR LIFE
A JOURNEY TO SPIRITUAL TRANSFORMATION

Copyright © 2016 by Josh Moody

Library of Congress Cataloging-in-Publication Data has been requested.

ISBN 978-1-5018-2484-5

The last part of the chapter "Sunday" is from a sermon by Josh Moody that was included in *Unashamed Workmen: How Expositors Prepare and Preach*, edited by Rhett Dodson and published in the Mentor imprint of Christian Focus Publications, Fearn, Ross-shire, Scotland, www.christianfocus.com, and is used with their kind permission.

16 17 18 19 20 21 22 23 24—10 9 8 7 6 5 4 3 2 1

This one is dedicated to Josiah

Contents

ACKNOWLEDGMENTS

With thanks to:

Carolyn Litfin, my brilliant executive assistant, without whom things would be chaos, who ensures that what I write is expertly proofread, that I turn up on time where I am meant to be, and who generally somehow manages to fill in the gaps for all the details I regularly lose.

The staff team at College Church: it is a joy to labor together for the progress of the gospel. In particular, and by extraordinary emphasis, the gracious and Bible-teaching loving congregation of College Church. I love you and am glad that I can serve as your pastor. The team at God Centered Life Ministries: with gratitude for all the new movement of raising a generation of 18- to 30-year-olds to center their lives on God.

Steve Laube, literary agent extraordinaire: what a gift you are to me. The good people at Abingdon: you are a joy to work with, and I am thrilled by your professional attention and the emphasis you have given to this book. Lisa Cook, Matt Litfin, Michael McKittrick, Curt Miller, Kyle Mueller, Tim Onufrock, and Anna Marie Wachs, who graciously provided feedback on the earliest manuscript.

Trinity Baptist, those years together were extraordinarily

blessed. Eden Baptist for the years running the growing student ministry. Pat Blake for your encouragement, support, and wise counsel for Rochelle and me. St. Andrew's the Great: the Church of England church where the rector, Mark Ashton, and the student worker, Jem Hovil, taught, mentored, shaped, invested in me. CICCU for giving me an opportunity to lead. Phil Parker for mentoring me and tutoring me on two ways to live. Lymington Camps for giving me opportunity to lead and teaching me how to teach. IFES, for allowing me and the team to go off and pioneer the gospel.

Thank you to the endorsers for endorsing this work with more kindness than I deserve. David Dockery for being a brilliant example of what honored, gracious, extremely savvy, wise, great Christian servant-leadership looks like. Phil Ryken for standing with us in the gap in his excellent leadership at Wheaton College. John Piper for giving me the best bit of midlife advice I have ever heard. Bruce Howard for his frequent wise counsel. Roger Sandberg for his encouragement, wisdom, and belief in me. The C. S. Lewis Institute in Chicago for their regular ongoing partnership in the gospel. Mark Dever for encouraging me as an undergraduate student. Don Carson for wise counsel and for his regular, ongoing, international class leadership, vision, teaching, and wisdom. Curtis Cook and Robert Krumrey: On the Border conversations that keep me on the straight and narrow. Jay Ridenour: I'd go into battle with you. Collin Hansen for featuring me in Young, Restless, Reformed and for giving me a key moment of counsel when I was wrestling with a call to a new church. Dennis Hollinger for his expert leadership, encouragement, and friendship.

My parents: mum and dad, you have been an unfailing example of sane, godly, "normal," humble, and remarkably intelligent Christian maturity. My brothers: Sam and George, we wrestled together and shaped life together. My children: Josiah, Sophia, Elianna, Elijah, you are my joy, my love, and I believe in you. Most of all to Rochelle: besides God, you are my rock.

7 Days

Seven days you shall eat unleavened bread, and on the seventh day there shall be a feast to the LORD.

—Exodus 13:6

The city is situated between two juts of rock, helpfully called East Rock and West Rock. On the flat plane beneath these two small hills, the houses and roads span out to the coast, and from the top of either West or East Rock, you can look down and see the city spread before you, reaching out to the sea. When you are in the city, you would hardly know that it was on the edge of the coastline, but when you are up high and look out, you are reminded that the city is a coastal city indeed. East Rock is more populated, is easier to access, and tends to be filled with crowds of holidaymakers and families having picnics. West Rock is more remote. It is usually quieter. You have to walk.

One day (I think it was a Monday), I hiked to the top of West Rock. My life had been unusually busy for a season, and this in a lifestyle that over the years had gradually developed to being more than normally busy as a normal pattern of life. But not only had I pushed the pedal down faster and more aggressively for longer than was probably wise, and hence was tired, I had come to a crossroads in my life. Somewhere inside I knew it, though I'm not sure I could have articulated it that way.

The reasons for this crossroads are boring and personal, and I don't want to break the rule of Too Much Information as I share, but I do somehow want to set the context for this book. It comes out of a long experience of talking with people as their pastor and finding that the resource/book I wanted to give them did not seem to exist. So as I discovered that there was a need for a book like the one in your hands, I wondered whether I should write it. That was the origin of the book, but the book did not really get going until it got personal. Like Augustine's *Confessions*, there is a need in Christian literature for not only objective reporting of the biblical facts but also openhearted and scarily honest engagement with those facts.

I have no desire to be weak; in fact, I think I am strong by most people's standards. I am a jock (as Americans call it), a games player (as the English say), and one who always gave himself, at least from the teenage years, to equally strenuous mental pursuits. I think most people would look at my life and think I have achieved much—a PhD, a successful church planting, and senior pastor of a large, well-known church—but at this point in my life to which I am referring, I became more acutely aware of my own weakness than at any other time before or since.

I am encouraged that the apostle Paul teaches us that when

we are weak, we are strong. But that's probably just my male macho side insisting on being heard: I want to tell you I was weak, but I have to tell you that that was really strong! How complex we all are.

This crossroads moment was related to my son. Given that he may one day read these words, I will say no more than that he was diagnosed with severe medical issues, suffering physically as well as mentally from autism, is now doing extraordinarily well, will probably outearn us all, and will achieve great things. I trust that he knows how much he has been used by God to change this arrogant high achiever into some sort of vessel that God might be able to use a little bit. I had nowhere else to go, so (late as ever) I went to God.

As I sat close to the precipice of West Rock, I realized that I was not really at a crossroads; instead, I was at a cliff's edge. Suddenly I realized that God had given his Son for me. Hardly news, you might say, but it hit me like a rocket-propelled grenade, and it opened the tear ducts like an English public schoolboy is never meant to admit. I wanted my son to be fixed; I couldn't understand why God wouldn't; I realized that God had intended, deliberately, to have his Son be unfixed, crucified, fixed to a cross. Hard as it is to watch your own son suffering and not be able to do anything about it, what would it be like to watch your own Son suffering, be able to stop it, but deliberately not do so for the sake of your love for the others for whom he dies?

That thought began a new search for a resource/book that would help others come to a point of starting again. You don't have to be in crisis. You just have to want to be revitalized.

Who doesn't? If you don't, I'm a little bit worried for you, to be honest. It's a bit like humility: if you don't think you need to work on your humility, you can be sure you most definitely do. If you don't think you need a new (or renewed) work of God in your life, then you may need it all the more.

WHAT IS DISCIPLESHIP?

I've structured this book around seven days, partly for simplicity and ease of use but also for biblical reasons. The biblical idea, which this book pushes throughout all of its pages and every single day, is that discipleship is fundamentally about following Jesus. Discipleship is not just about learning some techniques or getting certain patterns of behavior right. Discipleship is responding to Jesus' call, "Come, follow me," with a yes and then *actually following him*. Obviously, that can (and does) include certain disciplines or spiritual practices, but much more than that, it requires a new relationship to your past and a new relationship to your future. For Jesus to call you to "Come, follow me" means for you to stop whatever you were doing and wherever you were going (past), and start going wherever he's going and doing whatever he's doing (future). This call is not individualistic; it is not just "you and Jesus" so that you forget about everyone else. The call goes out not only to you but also to many others down through history, across cultures, all around the globe, on into the future. You, as you

> Jesus looks at *you* and sees *you* and loves *you* and wants *you* to come and follow him.

follow Jesus, are part of the new people of God, the new "twelve tribes," which the twelve disciples signify (Matthew 19:28), and a part, therefore, of the New Testament church. There is a new relationship to God that comes about as a result of following Jesus, which means a new relationship to others who are also following Jesus—that is, to the true, biblical, New Testament church.

So discipleship is a community project, but that does not mean that it is impersonal either. It is not *merely* "you and Jesus," but it certainly starts there. Jesus looks at *you* and sees *you* and loves *you* and wants *you* to come and follow him. The call of discipleship, then, is at its most basic a change of relationship to the past, and a change of relationship to the future, a journey that others who are following Jesus also take but that *you yourself* are called to take in following Jesus.

There is an underlying logic to the New Testament call to discipleship, which can be helpfully summarized in two Greek words: *metanoia* and *mysterion*. *Metanoia* is the word usually translated "repent," but which has the sense of "change your mind." *Metanoia* is the switch from one way of thinking and behaving to another way of thinking and behaving. The translation "repent" is perfectly valid, but it can have overtones of "do penance," a Latin word that for the typical English reader conjures up pictures of "penitential" activity, certain good deeds that have to be done to make up for the bad deeds, or in the very worst of this mistaken mental picture of the word, it can mean things like beating yourself (and therefore can mean beating yourself up psychologically, as few people reach for a discipline rod anymore physically to do penance). No, *metanoia* is both more difficult than that and also far less sinister. It simply means to stop thinking one set of things about Jesus, and to start thinking another set of things about Jesus. Its cousin is faith; repentance and faith are seldom found very separate in the Bible. "Repent and believe" are the R & B (rhythm and blues) of gospel Christianity.

That said, *mysterion* connects more in New Testament thinking to *what* is believed. We get the word *mystery* from *mysterion*, but like the misconceptions we can have with what *metanoia* means, that interpretation can almost be as bad. Mystery tends to mean a problem that needs to be solved, a whodunit piece of literature, or a mystery crime in the newspapers that remains baffling. Or *mystery* can connect to the idea of "mysterious" or "mystical," thereby meaning something weird or even thrilling.

But *mysterion* in the New Testament almost always develops into a technical term meaning "that which was hidden but has now been revealed in the gospel of Jesus Christ." So marriage is a mystery, not in the sense of "who on earth can ever figure out how to make this marriage thing work?" but in the sense that right from creation it was a mystery, a God-given hint intended to point to what would be revealed, that is "Christ and the church" (Ephesians 5:32). The *mysterion* of the gospel is how much Jesus loves us, how much he "gave himself up" for us; it is centered on Christ's death and resurrection.

That's why structuring this book around the number seven is partly practical organization for the sake of simplicity and ease of use but also coherently biblical. Seven is a number used frequently in Scripture, and in Matthew's Gospel Jesus calls disciples to "Follow me" seven times, and each time he journeys closer to Calvary, nearer the cross. Discipleship, then, is "leaving and cleaving"; it is leaving the past, stopping being stuck (*metanoia*), and following Jesus to the cross (*mysterion*), and thereby a new and changed life.

HOW IS THIS BOOK GOING TO HELP?

It's going to give you a focal point—a biblical, gospel-centered, Christ-honoring focal point. For seven days, it will call you away from the past and toward the future, away from the self and toward God, away from sin and to salvation, away from habits and evil behavior that enslave and damage you and toward freedom and liberty, away from the pettiness and the boring life this world offers and toward transcendence and excitement and also suffering and sacrifice for the sake of Jesus.

It's structured around these seven days. We will be looking at the seven "Follow me" statements from Matthew's Gospel, one each day, starting Monday. But as the number seven is the number of perfection in the Bible, there are various places where biblical teaching is wrapped around this number seven. We'll look at some of those places as well, which also bear on this matter of revitalization and discipleship. There is nothing mystical about seven! There is no "hidden meaning" to seven, but the Bible does use it in a few instances as an organizing principle that reverberates with the divine completion, which was first proclaimed when he had finished all his work of creating and deemed it "very good."

Then there are seven signs given in John's Gospel, each of

which is intended to help us believe in Jesus. On top of that, we will also look at the seven "I Am" statements in John's Gospel, which are declarations from Jesus of who he is, in what sense he is the Great "I AM," the One True God. Finally, there are seven letters from Jesus to the churches of Asia, in the first chapters of Revelation, which will conclude each of the seven days.

Unleavened Bread

In order to make the most of these seven days, set aside the time in a formal fashion. There is no legalism here; you can read the book any which way you like, though usually starting at the beginning is best. But you can dip in, dip out, do one day (Tuesday), wait a week, come back and do another (Wednesday), and so on. You don't *have* to do it all in seven consecutive days, but it will probably help if you do. You could do it with others in a small group. You could do it as a church. Start Monday, and move all the way to Sunday. Of course, Monday is, in a sense, really the second day of the week, but again there's no legal structure to this book at this level beyond what would be helpful. While Sunday (as the Lord's Day) is the first day of the week, of the New Creation, of Redemption, it is also the eternal Day of the Resurrection, and it seems perfectly fitting to conclude there as much as to start there.

So, you don't have to set aside a particular week to read this book, but if you do, take on board the idea of "unleavened bread" from the Book of Exodus used in the quotation at the start of this introduction. God's people were being set free from

Egypt, their life of bondage and slavery was going to be completed, and to commemorate this moment, they were asked to remember it in a feast of Passover, followed then by the feast of unleavened bread, which would last for...seven days.

In the New Testament the idea of "unleavened bread" is used at times to tell us to rid ourselves of the sin that so easily entangles. The leaven, or yeast, stands as a metaphor, a picture, for sin that can spread throughout the batch of dough, the bread that is going to be baked, throughout our lives, and throughout the community. You can see "unleavened" bread used this way by Paul, for instance, in his teaching about sin in 1 Corinthians 5:7. Christ is the Passover Lamb; he has been sacrificed, so let us celebrate this new feast, the ongoing feast of following Jesus, by cleansing out the "leaven of malice and evil" and replacing it with "the unleavened bread of sincerity and truth" (1 Corinthians 5:8).

> All Christian revitalization comes down to answering that divine command of the Messiah with the first step of faith.

So to get ready for this week, whether you do it in a literal week or not, take the time to get rid of the leaven of malice and evil. There is no point in "just going through the motions" of revitalization, of commitment to follow Jesus, while holding on to old patterns and beliefs. There is a need for a *metanoia*. This can be hard. This is gradual. Don't worry; the theme will run through the book. If it's any encouragement, those who think they don't have any malice and evil probably have the most (we're back to the analogy with humility again, I suppose).

But whereas in the New Testament the metaphor is picked up as referring to sin ("malice and evil"), in the Old Testament the unleavened bread, at the Exodus, was at first connected with simplicity. The whole point was speed. They shall eat the sacrificed lamb, and the unleavened bread, with bitter herbs, *fast*. "In this manner you shall eat it: with your belt fastened, your sandals on your feet, and your staff in your hand. And you shall eat it in haste" (Exodus 12:11). Unleavened bread was quicker to bake, lighter to carry, easier to move quickly with.

Such simplicity, a streamlined approach to the week, is also important. It is going to require focus. There is nothing wrong with watching television or surfing the Internet. There is nothing wrong with texting, blogging, or being plugged into an MP3 player or iPod or the equivalent. But part of the slavery of modern life is the constant demand of e-mail, text, the siren voice of the TV in the corner of the living room, the gaming station, and all the rest. Turn it off.

I know that when you are at work, you're going to need to respond to e-mails and surf the Internet. Fine.

But when you're home, when you are reading this, turn it off. The whole lot. Every bell, whistle, beep, buzz, and ringtone. Unleavened bread.

A Day for Hope

And he said to them, "Follow me, and I
will make you fishers of men."

—*Matthew 4:19*

The movie *Prince Caspian* describes a world that has run out of hope. An evil dictator rules the world. The oppressed Narnians are hiding in the forest, away from the watching eyes of the soldiers, and Caspian himself, meant to be the next king, is in danger because his wicked uncle now has an heir. He must also go into hiding. His tutor puts him on a horse in the dead of night and gives him a few supplies—and one great magic instrument: a horn. Susan's magic horn, rediscovered from old times, now a horn to blow in his greatest need, a horn that never fails to find help when hope is lost.

The movie and C. S. Lewis's book have some details that are different, but for our purposes, the point is the same: this horn stands as a symbol of hope. Caspian blows the horn when he is knocked off his horse (movie) or when they are besieged by the enemy at Aslan's How (book), and in either case the response is straightaway, though Caspian has to wait to find out who his rescuers will be. The call goes out, and Peter, Lucy, Susan, and Edmund are called out of their world into the world of Narnia to rescue the Narnians.

Similarly, God's rescuers have often appeared in response to his people's prayers, not a magic horn, but prayer is a more powerful instrument in God's hands. When the Hebrews were in slavery in Egypt, God sent them Moses when he heard their prayers for help. Moses was a man who had grown up among them, a "prince of Egypt," driven away by his own sense of guilt, and then many years later called back by God to be his way of saving his people. He had heard his people groaning, and Moses was sent. Then there is the story of God's rescuers in the Book of Judges, which tells of twelve champions sent in response to the blowing of the spiritual horn of prayer. None of these champions are perfect by any means, and some do deeds that would shock us. Their weaknesses are displayed as much as their strengths, and yet in their weaknesses God uses them to rescue his people, as they cry out again and again for help. That is the pattern: sin, rebellion, crying out to God, then a savior (or champion) is sent. Yet, rescuers though they are, none of them are the Rescuer. All of this story, and more, is preparation for God's true Rescuer, the Savior, "Aslan" himself: Jesus Christ, who comes into the world to lighten our darkness. And when he comes he says—seven times in Matthew—"Follow me."

What I have discovered in my own journey is that in the most profound sense possible, all Christian revitalization comes down to answering that divine command of the Messiah with the first step of faith. "Follow me," Jesus says, and if we say yes and begin to do so, we will begin to find hope.

BURYING THE PAST

It is interesting that both the Narnians and the Pevensies (the four children in *Prince Caspian*) had lost hope. The Pevensies were bored or frustrated, and they had given up hope that they would ever go back to Narnia, that place of adventures and dreams and greatness. They had been there once before, but would they ever return? We think of our spiritual heroes as carved out of granite, but sometimes they are as much in need of rescuing people as people are in need of being rescued. I don't mean the "messiah syndrome," where people feel they have to help others when really they are the ones who need help themselves. And I don't mean to suggest that the divine Jesus—begotten not made, of one being with the Father—*needs* anything at all.

Still, he did lament unrepentant Jerusalem, and he wept at the tomb of Lazarus, and however you put together the Immutability of God philosophically with the passion of Christ at the cross, clearly our Savior *wants* us, even if he cannot be said to *need* us. What can the infinite, the eternal, the divine lack? Answer: nothing. Yet the love of God is poured out, and it is the very nature of Godhead (Philippians 2 would suggest) to give, to serve, to bend down, to love. We should worship the Great God of the Universe, and that means we should follow Jesus specifically, not simply make him Providence, the Deity, or (worse) Fate.

Of course, the true need is on our side of the equation. It is an unequal covenant that God has established with us, a covenant purely of grace, where it might be said that he has everything and we simply need everything. We respond with faith, to be sure, and we are to keep our side of the bargain with faithful obedience. But God's covenant with us was a one-sided covenant, a bit like a man who provides all the food at a party and where everyone else's job is to eat it. It's all by grace, even if that grace needs to be worked out with fear and trembling, with active obedience on our part. From the beginning, this covenant in the Old Testament was guaranteed by God himself, passing through halves of animals in a symbol that would have been familiar to covenant makers and breakers of the ancient world, meaning that that is what would happen to them if the covenant were broken (Genesis 15:7-21). He passed through the symbolically halved pieces alone because it is he who is the foundation for such an audacious, outlandish, expensively gracious promise to sinners like us. He guarantees the covenant by his promise and his person, and ultimately it costs him his Son's death on the cross.

What that means is that hope cannot come until we bury the past. And that can only successfully be accomplished when what must be buried is first dead. We all have different backstories that, uninterred, can haunt us like ghosts in our minds. But for every one of us there is a single source of that pain that must die and be buried. Sin. That three-letter word that some churches fear to mention in case their attendees will find other churches that do not mention it. Every revitalization is a following of Jesus, and following Jesus means no longer following whatever it is you were following. We emulate a variety of human ideals, aspire to a legitimate range of exemplary roles, but in ultimate terms following anything other than Jesus is following sin. It's darkness, hopelessness; it's sitting on the train platform, bored out of your mind, hoping for some excitement and adventure today; it's sitting in a castle, scared out of your mind because some wicked uncle has you under his control; it's hiding in a forest, reverting to dumb animals because the image of God in us is being replaced by purely animal-like desires of survival and pleasure, not greatness and hope.

One of the distinguishing aspects of the Christian story is that it is a story of hope. If we follow Jesus, we get to be a part of that good thing. There are secular versions of hope too: the Manifest Destiny and the American Dream, but the good ones of these tend to be a secularization of the Christian one. They are the Christian story of life going somewhere good but without Christ and God. They are the story without the hero of the story, and ultimately they tend to disappoint and become cynically hopeless as well if they are not rooted in Christ.

"Follow me," Jesus says. Don't follow religion; don't follow rules; don't follow what other people have always told you to do. Repentance, which sounds like such a harsh word in our understanding of it today, is *metanoia*, changing your mind, what comes after the old mind-set, and so is prepared now to think differently and so believe and act differently. That Greek word was translated in the Latin version of the Bible as "do penance," and since then has often in Western culture had the sense of doing something nasty to yourself. But really it is hope. It is no longer following what bedevils you and

> The work of the Spirit in our lives is like new wine being poured into new wineskins.

beginning to follow no one but Jesus.

One of the tricky things about this for Narnians who grew up in Christian homes and feel like they've heard the old, old story many times before and have become a little tired of it is feeling that any of this is new. We are familiar with the traditional answers and are happy for them, but we are still hiding in our forest, away from the wicked uncle on the throne, doing our own thing but without much of a dream for a new day of hope to dawn.

Tradition is a hard matter to write about because by its very nature it is varied. My tradition is not yours, and yours is not mine, and your neighbor's is dissimilar again. I am always suspicious of people who throw off all tradition on the basis of the argument that "the world is changing" because in every age that has ever existed, people have said that the world is changing. As ancient Aristotle was said to have remarked, "When I look at the next generation, I fear for the future of the world."

Tradition can be wonderfully helpful, even hopeful, because it tells us that people have come before us and we can learn from them and build on the shoulders of giants. But it can also be a ball and chain. It just depends what the tradition that is yours teaches you.

That's why I say follow Jesus and let your tradition be judged by that, and not the other way around. Does Jesus eat with sinners? Then you are to do so as well. Does Jesus care for the poor? Then you are to do so as well. We need precision here, of course, because Jesus also turned water into wine, walked on water, and died for the sins of the world, and none of us is able to do any of those things. Following Jesus does not merely mean "What Would Jesus Do?" (WWJD) in that simplistic sense; it means "What Does Jesus Teach?" (WDJT). That's why we are looking at these seven commands of Jesus, in context, in Matthew's Gospel, to see what he teaches us to do.

And first is the initial command to follow him, which means stopping following other things, which means beginning to bury the past or at least to leave it behind. Hope starts with leaving. The adventure of Middle-earth begins when we leave our hobbit hole. As J. R. R. Tolkien said, "It's a dangerous business, Frodo, going out of your door. You step onto the road, and if you don't keep your feet, there is no knowing where you might be swept off to."[1]

The Future Is Bright

Jesus' command to follow him comes right away with a promise of what he will do: "I will make you fishers of men." We will look at what "fishers of men" means in a moment, but at the beginning of that phrase Jesus tells us that following him means something good about the future. There is something that he is going to do for us, with us, to us, that will be good.

The future is so bright, sang a rock band of the 1980s, I gotta wear shades. Wonderful cynicism glancing toward those who promise overly positive, feel-good outcomes. When I say the future is bright, I am not saying that you are never going to have any troubles again, that you will be able to pay off your mortgage, that you won't get cancer, that you will never have an argument with your spouse again. I am saying that Jesus is promising something good, and what that good is we will think about in a moment (= "fishers of men").

But it's important, in this week of personal revitalization, to take time to soak in the idea that Jesus has an agenda that is bright about our future. There are lots of ways that the Bible underlines this for us, and one of them is with the miracles that Jesus does—not just healings but signs of a bigger, better future that will be ours.

Take the first of the seven signs that John describes in his Gospel: Jesus turning the water into wine. I've read the commentaries and studied the text, and while I understand the argument that Jesus turned the water into unfermented grape juice, I still do not believe it. There's a bigger picture here that we need to grasp, which is that wine is a symbol of the hope of the new kingdom, of God's redeeming work in this world. God's people are a vineyard. The work of the Spirit in our lives is like new wine being poured into new wineskins. Certainly, wine in the ancient world was not the 40-proof alcohol of hard liquor, nor was it the very strong wines of some vintages today, but it was without question alcoholic because the reason for it was to provide a source of safe drinking water that would not kill you. The original purpose of the fermentation, distilling, and all the rest, was to make the water safe to drink. An unexpected side effect was that it tasted good. Such is God, and such is hope.

God is in the business of turning your water into wine. I don't mean that you have to start drinking alcohol if you would rather not; to paraphrase Paul, I would never drink again if it caused my brother or sister to stumble. It is a message, a sign pointing in a certain direction that is intended to make us look at the thing it is pointing to and not at the sign itself. The water-turned-to-wine miracle is not meant to make us scratch our heads about how Jesus did it or what he meant when he said to his mother, "Woman, what does this have to do with me?" (see John 2:4). We are meant to look at the sign and then go where it is pointing. If the sign says, "New York 50 miles," then we start looking toward New York and expect to get there in fifty miles or an hour or so, depending on traffic. We don't pull off the highway, examine the paint, think about the lettering of the sign, wonder how deep the sign went into the ground, and start to build our own little signs ourselves. We keep on going; we go where the sign is pointing.

Your life with Jesus, then, is meant to be like wine, not like water. That is, it's meant to have flavor; it's meant to taste good; it's meant to be beyond the normal and everyday. It's meant to make you truly happy ("wine that makes glad the heart of man," Psalm 104:15 NKJV), not in an alcoholic buzz way, and certainly not by drunkenness, nor in a giddy, superficial, Let's-just-clap-our-hands-and-put-on-a-fake-smile way. But wine, not water.

PURPOSE

A big part of this is the purpose that it gives us. "Follow me," Jesus says, "and I will make you fishers of men." Jesus has a particular purpose for these early disciples, and while that purpose may be in some ways different for us than it was for them, there is an overlap. When in the past they were fishers of fish, now they have become fishers of people. Their task now is to "catch" people—not to move them, as with fish, from life to death but to move them, as with people, from death to life. The rest of the Bible makes it clear that not all of us are to abandon our nets or our personal businesses, our homes, our native countries or cities. Most of us are to earn a living, to provide for our families, to look after those nearest to us, and to love our neighbors. But even if, unlike them, we are meant to stay with the nets physically, none of us is meant to stay focused on the nets as the end point, a fishing business without a purpose.

Our fishing is to be for the ultimate goal of people fishing. Certainly, fishing itself has value, but fishing is given purpose by Jesus as a vehicle for honoring him, loving him, and pointing others to him. Everything we do we can do for God. Work for the Lord. Work is a form of worship. Caring for children is a form of worship. And now, with Jesus, it all has purpose. It's part of a future that is going somewhere; it means something because it's for Someone. Work is not only an evangelistic opportunity; work is work and, done for God, is worship.

But work for Jesus (Fishers of Men) now reverberates with meaning that others will see, if they have eyes to see, and does, God willing, provide opportunities not simply to fish for fish but fish for the people with whom you are fishing; not simply build corporations but build up people with whom you are working; not simply heal physical ailments but help people find spiritual healing.

This is not what some people call Platonic dualism; that is, we are not saying that the physical is less important than the spiritual or that the secular working world is less important than religious work. This is fishing for Jesus; it has purpose to it all.

You can tell a lot about a culture by the visions it has about its future. If you go back and read the futuristic visions of H. G. Wells and the early pioneers of this craft, you will find that they often had a vision of an ongoing progress of humanity. Everything changed for that generation after World War I. Beforehand, Wells had viewed the uninterrupted development of humanity harnessed to science as a near certainty, and he was happy to give it imaginative life through his creative speculations about the future. But after the carnage of war, he viewed the dark side of humanity as soiling any possible future visions.

Afterward came the dystopian future visions of Aldous Huxley's *Brave New World* or George Orwell's *1984*. These stories were darker and dismal; the future was certainly not bright, and it was dominated by massive inhuman bureaucratic states controlling the individuals according to what would best feed the machine of the government. Now our visions of the future are not just depressing; they are horrific. In the *Terminator* movies, Sarah and John Connor are constantly fighting against an impending apocalypse, and we seem to feel that we are at the mercy of technology getting out of our control and leading toward a brave new world that is terrifying and destructive, even damning. Some of us may even feel that right now we are in the control of some hidden global elite, an illuminati, who are feeding off our personal lives, dreams, and energies by some horrible *Matrix*-like machine. It has been a long time since a positive, purposeful view of the future, of any kind at all, was put together, even of the likes of *2001: A Space Odyssey*.

When Jesus comes and points us away from the past and to the future, what he is really doing is pointing us to himself. He is the Alpha and the Omega, the first and the last, the beginning and the end, and all hopes and dreams are met in him. Not only does John have seven signs, in his Gospel he also records Jesus giving seven "I Am" statements, the last repeated twice for emphasis. Each of these is metaphorical, using picture language, to describe who Jesus is. Jesus talks about himself as "I Am" elsewhere in John's Gospel too, but these seven metaphorical descriptions paint pictures of who he is. When Jesus says simply "I Am," he is probably telling us he is *the* "I AM," the four-letter Old Testament description of God, YHWH ("Yahweh"). When he uses metaphor or picture language, he is describing vividly what this means, with particular reference to him being the fulfillment of God's salvation plan, the Messiah.

The first of these "I Am" statements in John's Gospel comes in John 6:35: "I am the bread of life." Jesus has just fed five thousand people out of a few loaves, and now they have come looking for him, and he is telling them that he, not the physical bread, is the real focus. "I am the bread of life; whoever comes to me shall not hunger, and whoever believes in me shall never thirst." The fact that Jesus "mixes" the metaphor of eating with that of drinking tells us that we are not to push the literal meaning of these metaphors too far. As the bread of life, Jesus is far more than even Moses, through whom God gave his people manna from heaven in the desert.

Jesus is the bread of life, meaning he is the purpose of

life even beyond our physical needs and providing for our bodily sustenance. That's quite a claim, and what it tells us is not that Jesus does not care about people's physical needs (he's just fed five thou-

> Somehow, for some reason, he has poured this glory (and love) and grace into us.

sand people), nor that Jesus thinks that spiritual things are more important than bodily (he will be raised bodily from the dead). What it means is that someone can sit in a prison cell for Jesus—starving, beaten, thirsty—and be singing hymns of praise without faking it. He or she can even be unemployed and have hope without faking it. The purpose of life is Jesus, not physical bread.

We, as it were, need to chew on that and think about it and inwardly digest it. The meaning of your life is not acquiring more and more "bread" or stuff or things or bigger houses or faster cars, or even faithfully doing a good job at work. Faithfully doing a good job is excellent for you and your household, but the meaning, the purpose of life, is Jesus himself.

POINT

If that is the purpose, what is the point? The typical Sunday school answer of the child to any question asked is "Jesus." And while we know that somehow he is indeed the beginning and end of everything, and what life is truly all about, if we don't dig a little deeper, saying only that Jesus is the purpose can feel pointless. One of the great mysteries over which the prophets and the apostles scratch their heads is that the point—in some shape or form—is Jesus' people. You and me. The church.

Paul calls this a mystery: "This mystery is profound, and I am saying that it refers to Christ and the church" (Ephesians 5:32). In a much larger survey of the gospel, for example in the epistle to the Christians in Rome, he comes to a similar conclusion: "Oh, the depth of the riches and wisdom and knowledge of God! How unsearchable are his judgments and how inscrutable his ways! 'For who has known the mind of the Lord, or who has been his counselor? Or who has given a gift to him that he might be repaid?' For from him and through him and to him are all things. To him be glory forever. Amen" (Romans 11:33-36). And then, with this ringing admiration and worship still echoing in the vaults of the Book of Romans, as a conclusion to his great panoply of God's salvation plan for Jew and Gentile, he begins chapter 12 with a "therefore" (a point): "I appeal to you therefore, brothers, by the mercies of God"— these mercies he has outlined in the gospel—"to present your bodies as a living sacrifice" (Romans 12:1).

The point is us. It is all for God and for his glory. Jesus is the purpose. But somehow, for some reason, he has poured this glory (and love) and grace into us. The appeal at the beginning of Romans 12 is not a guilt trip to get us to be good little boys and girls because "think about all he went through." It's saying, "All this is for us, so join in! Be a part of it!" God in Christ "did not count equality with God a thing to be grasped" because the very nature of God is self-giving (Philippians 2:6). God has always been a lover. And love requires sacrifice. And that sacrifice is for us. And the point is that we get to join in too.

The psalmists similarly scratch their heads over God's mercy. "What is man that you are mindful of him, and the son of man that you care for him? Yet you have made him a little lower than the heavenly beings and crowned him with glory and honor" (Psalm 8:4-5). How could it be that God, the Creator ("When I look at your heavens, the work of your fingers, the moon and the stars, which you have set in place" [Psalm 8:3]), takes any notice at all of us humans in particular? And how can it be that he has crowned us with glory, as his people, to be the point of his redemption for all eternity?

Isaiah 43 is perhaps the pinnacle of this thought in the Old Testament. Isaiah 40–55 tells of God's salvation plan: the suffering servant. Though "all we like sheep have gone astray," the "LORD has laid on him the iniquity of us all" (Isaiah 53:6). It rings with the hidden footfalls of the Messiah to come, with the prophetic brilliance that is the sure voice of Isaiah the man of God throughout. Yet in Isaiah 43, at the heart of this point, is us still: "For I am the LORD your God, the Holy One of Israel, your Savior. I give Egypt as your ransom, Cush and Seba in exchange for you" (v. 3). Why is this? How could it be that God would exchange whole powerful nations for the sake of his beloved people who in the New Testament age come from every nation? What is the reason for this, and what is the point? "Because you are precious in my eyes, and honored, and I love you, I give men in return for you, peoples in exchange for your life" (Isaiah 43:4).

Perhaps one of the most powerful ways to think about this focus that God has upon us as his people is to consider the seven days of creation. Each day has its own brilliant foray into the native genius of God. Each day is declared good; yet it is not until the sixth day that man and woman are created and after that day all is declared very good. The pinnacle of his creation is humanity, and the point of his salvation is his people.

Part, then, of finding hope on this first day of the week of revitalization is to focus not just on the purpose of it all, which is indeed Jesus, but also the point of that purpose, which is us. That is not in the slightest to detract from God's glory, for God has deemed it worthy to risk all (his very life) on our salvation, and so in his love and grace reveal his glory. This is not to detract from his glory; it is to emphasize it.

Neither is it in tension, one part with the other, as if God's glory and our good are at mutually opposite poles of reality. There is an authority in creating us as we are, in defining us as we are: for instance, in making us bound by the rules of gravity. And there is an authority in redeeming us and making us and pouring out God's glory upon us. When God says that we are his prized possession and that he loves us and when he breathes his new life into us, we are the point. But he is the purpose, the beginning and the end, the be-all and end-all of everything.

Whatever has happened to us in recent days or weeks, whatever our background, our family history, our personality, our psychological makeup, our gifts and our abilities; whatever, God is, he made us, he redeems us, he loves us, and he has a purpose for us of which we are the point. When we blow Susan's horn, the Pevensies are called; people are given "in exchange for your life" to redeem us because he loves us.

A powerful instance of this in practice is the novel and

movie *The Blind Side*. In football's professional development, it became increasingly important to be able to protect the "blind side" of the quarterback. Therefore, the position of left tackle, previously anonymous, gathered enormous value. Based on a true story, *The Blind Side* tells about one prosperous and privileged family who adopted an inner-city kid, loved on him, doted on him, and gave him an opportunity. Like an organism well planted and nourished, he began to bloom. He was blessed with remarkable size, strength, speed, and flexibility.

> Touched by Jesus! "Saying, 'Fear not, I am the first and the last, and the living one.'"

The story describes how this kid moved from an abusive and forgotten underclass to being one of the most successful football protégés of all time.

It's also laced with Christian values, such as the value of crossing cultural and financial barriers, the value of moving from the richer to the poorer, the value of grace, the values of mercy and kindness, the power of love, the desire to protect and serve. Certainly, football can be a violent and aggressive game, but in the midst of a game of ambitions, this young man's life—not just his abilities—became the point of the story. Likewise, with Jesus, WE are the point.

We live in a world where we increasingly feel so pointless. There are millions upon millions of people, and our lives do not seem to matter. We can fairly easily grab onto the idea that it's all about God and Jesus, but we feel unimportant.

Not to God.

Vision

At the end of each of these seven days, we are going to conclude with a letter from Jesus to the church. In the Book of Revelation, there are seven such letters. They were sent first to the beachhead city for the advance of the gospel in Asia, Ephesus, and from there couriered around the six other cities of the churches of Asia, which was then defined as the Roman province of Asia (now western Asia Minor). Ephesus was a great church, and you can read about its founding through the missionary work of the apostle Paul in Luke's Acts of the Apostles in the New Testament (Acts 19). It was for Ephesus that Paul gave his famous farewell to the Ephesian elders, laying down principles of Christian leadership in churches that have been used ever since (Acts 20). We also have Paul's letter to the Ephesians, where he describes in sublime profundity the teaching of the gospel, and calls on his readers to remember where they have come from and who saved them, in order to guide them as to how to act now as his church (Ephesians 2).

Then we come to the Ephesians at a later date, ready to receive their letter from Jesus. Imagine you were a part of that congregation in Asia, in the port city of Ephesus, and you were gathered together to find that a special letter had been sent to you from John from his exile on the Isle of Patmos, and that this was to be passed around the other churches of the province of Asia as well, with his strange apocalyptic Book of Revelation as the sequel to the letters from Jesus. You hear John's description of Jesus:

Then I turned to see the voice that was speaking to me, and on turning I saw seven golden lampstands, and in the midst of the lampstands one like a son of man, clothed with a long robe and with a golden sash around his chest. The hairs of his head were white, like white wool, like snow. His eyes were like a flame of fire, his feet were like burnished bronze, refined in a furnace, and his voice was like the roar of many waters. In his right hand he held seven stars, from his mouth came a sharp two-edged sword, and his face was like the sun shining in full strength. (Revelation 1:12-16)

Jesus, the purpose, like the sun shining in full strength. It is no wonder that John continues, "When I saw him, I fell at his feet as though dead." Yet, though he is the purpose, the glory, the power, with "eyes like a flame of fire," we are the point: "But he laid his right hand on me"—not to hurt or keep away, but to welcome and encourage. Touched by Jesus! "Saying, 'Fear not, I am the first and the last, and the living one. I died, and behold I am alive forevermore, and I have the keys of Death and Hades. Write therefore the things that you have seen, those that are and those that are to take place after this'" (Revelation 1:17-19).

Jesus' focus upon us as the point is shown in his touching, speaking, encouragement not to be afraid, and his emphasis upon his death and resurrection, which is to release us from death and hell, and from his giving us a written word. Jesus' first letter to the church at Ephesus follows. The seven stars in John's vision are the angels of the seven churches, and the seven lampstands are the seven churches themselves. And here is what Jesus writes in his first of seven letters to the churches:

To the angel of the church in Ephesus write: "The words of him who holds the seven stars in his right hand, who walks among the seven golden lampstands. I know your works, your toil and your patient endurance, and how you cannot bear with those who are evil, but have tested those who call themselves apostles and are not, and found them to be false. I know you are enduring patiently and bearing up for my name's sake, and you have not grown weary. But I have this against you, that you have abandoned the love that you had at first. Remember therefore from where you have fallen; repent, and do the works you did at first. If not, I will come to you and remove your lampstand from its place, unless you repent. Yet this you have: you hate the works of the Nicolaitans, which I also hate. He who has an ear, let him hear what the Spirit says to the churches. To the one who conquers I will grant to eat of the tree of life, which is in the paradise of God." (Revelation 2:1-7)

This is not the time or place to have a lengthy discussion about the various different sorts of interpretations that are possible for the Book of Revelation as a whole. Most good commentaries or study Bibles will help you have a sense of what the responsible options are. For our purposes, though, it is enough to say that the seven letters to the seven churches of Asia are historic documents written to actual churches with a message that spoke to them in their situation at the time. That does not mean it does not speak today; it does, like all of God's word, it is living and active and useful for us.

Now, the church of Ephesus, then, was clearly still a good

church. They had not grown weary. They believed the right things and resisted those who believed the wrong things. They were enduring. But despite this, they were missing an essential ingredient: they had lost the love they had at first. They needed to remember (what Paul had told them to do in his letter to the Ephesians years before, Ephesians 2:11-12), repent (in the sense we defined earlier, not being nasty to themselves but changing their viewpoint and their activity), and return to what they did at first. We are not sure exactly what specifically it is that Jesus meant by "what they did at first," though the Ephesian Christians would have known. But the principle is laid down that if we are losing our "first love," a passionate, glowing affection for Christ that newborn Christians experience, the solution is to go back and return to the kind of things we did when we had that love at first and before we took the false step toward cold, loveless routine.

Reading the Bible. Praying. Giving our money away to Christ's church. Telling other people about Jesus. Loving our neighbor. Loving God with all our hearts. The same is true for even human relationships: a love that is not what it was at first can be reignited by doing the things that such love would naturally do, and often the love itself will follow. Jesus does not want us to wait until we "feel" loving toward him, or other people, before we do loving things. He wants us to do loving things, and then find that we will feel loving afterward.

Imagine you received this letter from Jesus. There is much to commend: hard work, perseverance, believing the right things. Yet Jesus also holds out the hope of returning (revitalizing) to a time of more exuberant Christian life and love.

Sometimes the first step is the hardest, but it is also the most important. Blowing Susan's horn, making the decision to read this book, seeking revitalization. In Narnia, the talking animals and beasts had so long forgotten what it was like at first to be a free Narnian that some of them had even begun to forget how to talk at all. They needed to be awakened.

Sometimes it does not come without a fight. The devil and all his angels will do all they can to tell you that life now is all that there is, that you are just on the gentle slide down, and there is no return to hope and love and reawakening. When I think of the need to stand and fight, I am usually drawn in my mind to a speech of Winston Churchill's, perhaps his most famous of all his famous speeches: "We shall fight on the beaches."

The situation at the time of his speech was perhaps the most serious that any people could face. A large army was pinned with its back to the sea at the French port of Dunkirk, with a massive army facing it, disaster, death, and shame seemed the only possible result. And yet, certainly no victory, but a victory within a defeat (as Churchill suggested). There was, through the great and heroic bravery of many individuals, a flotilla of tiny ships from a small island, along with the fleet, that took soldiers alive, though with many individual losses, to fight again from the relative and temporary safety of the far shore.

Churchill described this chilling news to the British Parliament in a speech whose ending is rightly famous: "We shall fight on the seas and oceans, we shall fight with growing confidence and growing strength in the air, we shall defend our Island, whatever the cost may be. We shall fight on the beaches, we shall fight on the landing grounds, we shall fight in the fields and in the streets, we shall fight in the hills; we shall never surrender."[2]

We shall never surrender… delivered with Churchillian resolve.

What is seldom told in this story, which reaches mythic proportions (in English culture, at least), is that on hearing the news of the impending disaster, churches across the land were filled to the brim with pilgrims asking God to have mercy. Susan's horn?

The Second World War was one of those relatively tidy wars, when there was obvious evil on one side (Hitler) and the necessity of defense on the other. That does not hide the great ills that were committed by both sides, against civilians at times, and it does not (or should not) encourage nationalistic fever, or be used as an excuse for less morally clearcut combats. In many wars, people cry out to God from either side, but God is not party to our human jealousies and spite.

> The greatness of Jesus is in his personal condescension to want us to follow him.

Still, the words themselves, in the context… *we shall never surrender*. They encourage hope.

There is always hope if we follow Jesus. Revitalization begins with hearing the call of Jesus to follow him anew; that same call stopped the ancient disciples in their tracks and took them down a new path to make history. That call reaches out to us today in a fresh way, reverberating down through time as the authentic call of Jesus himself: "Follow me." It means putting things to one side that otherwise we would hang on to; the *metanoia* is a necessary part of the leaving, before we can cleave to Christ in a new way. But in Christ's call is the *mysterion* of the gospel, the mystery that is revealed in the person of Jesus himself walking off the pages of the dusty volume of an ancient book to look us in the eye, and say: "Follow me."

He does not tell us everything that it will mean straightaway; he does not map out for the early disciples (or for us) ten points that must be kept at all times, or three rules for the Christian life. The greatness of Jesus and his glory is in his personal condescension to look upon us and want us to follow him directly.

Augustine of Hippo offers us his call to "Follow me," in his *Confessions*:

> I now found myself driven by the torment in my breast to take refuge in this garden, where no one could interrupt that fierce struggle, in which I was my own contestant, until it came to its conclusion....I tore my hair and hammered my forehead with my fists; I locked my fingers and hugged my knees....
>
> I was held back by mere trifles, the most paltry inanities, all my old attachments. They plucked at my garments of flesh and whispered: "Are you going to dismiss us? From this moment we shall never be with you again, for ever and ever. From this moment you will never again be allowed to do this thing, or that, for evermore." What was it my God, when they whispered "This thing" or "that"? Things so sordid and so

shameful that I beg You in Your mercy to keep the soul of Your servant free from them....

I was asking myself these questions, weeping all the while with the most bitter sorrow in my heart, when all at once I heard the sing-song voice of a child in a nearby house. Whether it was the voice of a boy or a girl I cannot say, but again and again it repeated the refrain, "Take it and read, take it and read." At this I looked up, thinking hard whether there was any kind of game in which children used to chant words like these, but I could not remember ever hearing them before. I stemmed my flood of tears and stood up, telling myself that this could only be a divine command to open my book of Scripture and read the first passage on which my eyes should fall. For I had heard the story of Anthony, and I remembered how he had happened to go into a church while the Gospel was being read and taken it as a counsel addressed to himself when he heard the words: *Go home and sell all that belongs to you*....

So I hurried back to the place where Alypius [a best friend of Augustine] was sitting, for when I stood up to move away I had put down the book containing Paul's Epistles. I seized it and opened it, and in silence I read the first passage on which my eyes fell: *"Not in revelling and drunkenness, not in lust and wantonness, not in quarrels and rivalries. Rather, arm yourselves with the Lord Jesus Christ, spend no more thought on nature and nature's appetites."* I had no wish to read more and no need to do so. For in an instant, as I came to the end of the sentence, it was as though the light of confidence flooded into my heart and all the darkness of doubt was dispelled.[3]

So is Augustine's famous account of his conversion in his *Confessions*. This Monday you may not be starting for the first time (and Augustine himself had been brought up as a Christian); it may not feel like a conversion to you in a strict sense. But you may start again.

"Hope deferred makes the heart sick," Proverbs 13:12 says, "but a desire fulfilled is a tree of life." Tomorrow we're going to see how hope takes us to life.

A Day for Life

*And Jesus said to him, "Follow me, and leave the dead
to bury their own dead."*

—Matthew 8:22

In the sparsely populated forests of Afghanistan, a man is crying out for help. He is "bleeding out," as they say in medical terms; that is, his wound is in a main artery, and he is moments away from death as his heart pumps out his lifeblood onto the dry, sandy floor. He is also surrounded by the enemy and separated from his fellow soldiers, and there is a firefight going, with bustling, whistling, and thumping all around. He has done what he can with first aid, staunching the flow and applying pressure, but he still needs help, so he calls "Medic!"

For any of his comrades to move is to risk fairly certain death, or at least wounding too, and yet there is not a moment's hesitation from those around him, and rapidly another soldier responds to his fallen comrade's cry for help. He reaches him in time, and the man's life (this time) is saved.

Why people behave like this under the intense pressure of war has been the subject of many military studies down through the years, but the answer that comes back each time is similar. The man who is the hero does not consider his actions heroic. He did not even give his actions a second thought; he did it because it had to be done. Usually, there is no great consideration of the moral rights or wrongs of the cause for which they are fighting as the bullets thud around them; there is a bond, in life and for death, and on occasions, more often than we would think, that bond goes beyond human fears and courage to act at the risk of your own life.

Sebastian Junger, in his book titled simply *War*, goes with an entrenched group of soldiers to the front line of Afghanistan and experiences with them the boredom, the terror, the sheer randomness of fighting on the edge of sanity and the furthest reaches of American power and influence. He observes young men acting in ways not unlike the story I just told, caring for one another in great danger. The combat platoon with which he is embedded has a tradition of "blood out and blood in." When someone new arrives in the camp, that person is ceremonially beaten up by the rest of the team as a way of introduction; and when the person leaves, the same happens. Junger describes how this way of initiation is not changed even for a new commander; he too is blooded in before they accept him as part of the pack.

Jesus is elevating his discipleship above all other forms of following.

The word *pack*—my word, not Junger's—seems to be key

to understanding how and why people behave like this; that is, how and why they protect one another even at risk of their own lives. There is a bond, a covenant, if you like, which means that the one security that everyone has is that each would risk all to protect the other. But why is that bond there? Junger's answer is that the natural affinity of family ties is translated in the heat of battle to this group in the hinterland, the middle of nowhere, relying on nothing but themselves. They are, in their combat jargon, "brothers," and Junger thinks the jargon represents the deeper reality. They are family, and hence they die for one another and with one another.

I introduce Tuesday this way because Jesus' very radical second "Follow me" statement, of the seven in Matthew's Gospel, is often downplayed. The inference usually is that, in the ancient world, burial rituals were very long and arduous, and there is also the potential that the man's father was not even dead yet. So when the man asks permission from Jesus to stay and bury his father, what he is really doing is putting off the decision to follow Jesus indefinitely. He is saying, "I'll follow you, Jesus, when my family responsibilities are taken care of, when I've grown up and taken on the family business, when my father is safely provided for and I have made all the arrangements for his elderly care, and when he has gone the way of all the flesh and the funeral at great length is done, then I can come and follow you." But, of course, with that logic, as we all know, there will always be another responsibility that will demand the man's time. If not his father, then presumably his children who will require feeding and caring for and (in our terms) putting through college financially. And on it goes.

With this way of examining the well-known, controversial saying of Jesus, we are told that here is Jesus simply saying, "Don't put me off; don't wait; let's get on with it now."

I am sure there is much to this cultural context, and there may indeed be something to the possibility that the man's father is not yet dead. After all, it does indeed seem a little hard to swallow if the idea is that Jesus is saying, "Leave your father's corpse rotting on the side of the road and come and follow me." We know from elsewhere, to confirm this way of interpreting the text more lightly if you like, that Jesus is very strict about the need for us to perform family duties. The Pharisees did some quick-footed fake interpretation of Scripture that allowed someone to avoid looking after their aged parents (required by God's law) by declaring that the money for that purpose was actually a gift to God. So, in one cunning move, the Pharisees made more money for the Temple and released those who listened to them from unpleasant duties toward their parents.

Jesus denounced that as against God's word.

> For Moses said "Honor your father and your mother"; and, "Whoever reviles father and mother must surely die." But you say, "If a man tells his father or his mother, 'Whatever you would have gained from me is Corban'" (that is, given to God)—then you no longer permit him to do anything for his father or mother, thus making void the word of God by your tradition that you have handed down. And many such things you do. (Mark 7:10-13)

Jesus could not be clearer that his disciples must follow God's word in fulfilling their duties to their parents. Yet, here he says, "Leave your father unburied and come and fol-low me."

So I can understand why a cultural context is appealed to in order to explain this text more lightly. But it will not do, or not entirely so, because it is not only here that Jesus sets up loyalty toward him against loyalty toward family. "If anyone comes to me and does not hate his own father and mother and wife and children and brothers and sisters, yes, and even his own life, he cannot be my disciple" (Luke 14:26).

Once again, the traditional approach with this text is to say that what Jesus really means is something milder. When he says, "hate," he is using an ancient form of extreme speech to make a point. He is exaggerating; it is hyperbole, characteristic of Near Eastern Semitic language forms. No doubt this is true; Jesus is using hyperbole, and it is also no doubt true that Jesus is drawing a comparison. By the standard of the love we are to have for him, our appropriate affection and devotion to our families is to be so much less that someone watching might almost think we did not love them (which of course we do).

Nonetheless, this way of talking about life is all very different from our normal Christian way of speaking. You would hardly find a modern preacher saying these things even as hyperbole.

Jesus is elevating his discipleship above all other forms of following. When Jesus says, "Follow me, and leave the dead to bury their own dead," he is not just saying that he is more important than family loyalties. He is placing discipleship in the context of the Old Testament discipleship of the great prophets and saying that his discipleship is more important, and costs more, than even that.

Matthew 8 needs to be read in the context of 1 Kings 19:20, when Elijah, the great prophet, has called Elisha, his successor, to follow him. "And he [Elisha] left the oxen and ran after Elijah and said, 'Let me kiss my father and my mother, and then I will follow you.'" Elisha is asking for the chance to say good-bye to his parents before he begins his discipleship with Elijah. Elijah replies to Elisha, "Go back again, for what have I done to you?" Elisha returns to his father and mother, makes a good-bye meal out of the oxen, then having done so, sets off on his journey with Elijah.

Jesus, however, demands a still higher loyalty. When the man says, "Let me first go and bury my father," perhaps a request to stay with his family until the day of burial had come, Jesus simply replies, "Follow me, and leave the dead to bury their own dead." He is not just Elijah seeking an Elisha; he is the Lord calling a disciple, not merely another prophet, and so the disciples' response is correspondingly greater, as the Master is greater than all who have come before him (or since). Jesus is not asking us to abandon our families, and he is certainly not asking us to not respect our parents or care for our children or look after the aged or bury the dead literally, but he is asking us to follow him alone. Other responsibilities are now done in Jesus' name and for Jesus' honor and as a disciple of Jesus.

That is why the early Christian community began to refer to each other as "brothers and sisters." There was a recognition that loyalty to our earthly family echoed commitment to our heavenly Father, through faith in Jesus Christ, with whom and in whom we are all brothers and sisters together. And as all is for Jesus, as disciples of Jesus, we will be better brothers and sisters, husbands and wives, mothers and fathers than we would otherwise: Jesus' disciples will not forget his divine commands to care for their relatives. As Paul says, we are worse than the pagans if we do not even look after our family. But our worship is no longer the family; our worship is Jesus, and from him come our family responsibilities.

And it is not by accident that the point of tension centers on the ceremony of death. Families are bound together by many ties, but key among them is the concern to be there for each other when facing death and to carry on the family legacy after death. Blood, they say, is thicker than water. This saying was demonstrated by a horrible reality during the terrible slaughter of Rwanda, the center of what was the heartland of the East African Revival. Loyalties to family and extended family had so trumped loyalty to the moral affection and love for Christ, and therefore charity to all, that baptized believers felt somehow able to act in barbarous ways to those not their relatives. The blood of the tribe seemed thicker than the water of baptism.

This must not be so, not if we follow Jesus and let the dead bury their own dead. We do not so worship the family, or the tribe, that family feuds can spill over to bloody warfare. We worship Jesus alone. We love and care for our family, as well as those who are not from our blood family but who equally need Christian charity.

I have called this chapter, this Tuesday, "A Day for Life" because in calling us to follow him and let the dead bury their own dead, Jesus is calling us to an adventure, a life, a reality beyond the normal round of family duties and responsibilities. "I came," he says in John 10:10, "that they may have life and have it abundantly." If we follow Jesus, and let the dead bury their own dead, we are still taking an enormous risk. But that is a large part of the great attraction of being a disciple of Jesus, of being someone who follows him through the seven callings, to no longer be overshadowed by this world's fears of death and family genetic ties. Instead, we are moving to a reality that includes a far greater and more thrilling calling. Family life is governed by the three activities of birth, provision, and transition from one generation dying to the next, and even without faith in God, family is still a wonderful blessing and a foundation for society. But it is insufficient to generate true life, the life abundant that Jesus talks about. As mentioned earlier, we see the necessity of some sort of "family" with the young men the world over who gravitate to the thrill of frontline war, and form bands of brotherhood and family-like gangs, around a search for adventure.

But there is no life—and no adventure—like following Jesus.

BORED

Of course, many Christians, or "Narnians," as we called them in the previous chapter, are bored. They feel that the old stories of Cair Paravel and the legends handed down to them for generations may be true, but the stories and legends seem to make very little difference to their daily lives, the grind of Monday to Friday, or the excitement (or not) of the weekend.

Near where I live there is a home that I have dubbed in my mind "the Castle" because it looks a bit like a scaled-down version of a medieval European-style castle. I love castles and remember with great eagerness my first foray into the world of the different kinds of castles that Europe produced: the moats, the high-end castle called the concentric castle, and more. A visit to a castle in England is a visit to a forgotten world of glamour and medieval chivalry, or so the schoolchild in all of us wishes to believe. In reality castles were the powerhouses of the government, the forts and embattlements of the controlling or conquering army of the time. Nonetheless, we can all understand why someone might want to make his or her home as enormous as a castle, and in the style of a castle. It is fantastic, literally, a little bit of fantasy and romance brought into the run-of-the-mill world of everyday life.

Right now this local "castle" has a sign outside of it that indicates it is for sale, and it may well proceed at a fast rate to close, or it may sit there for some time, waiting for the right buyer. Somehow a castle for sale says something to me symbolically about where many of our purely earthly hopes and dreams, fantasies and desires, end up; we build them, we envision them, we create them, and at the end they have a little For Sale sign outside of them. Death comes to us all, and while memorials may give us the impression that our life will continue after we have gone, we are still dead and not there to enjoy the hoped-for stream of visitors to the gravestone. Family can carry on our names and

God loves everyone just as they are, full of sin, darkness, and evil.

carry our biological data in their genes, but we are not there to observe our grandchildren or great-grandchildren because we are still dead, after all.

Great political achievements, poetry, literature, music—"castles" all—can, we hope, pass on to future generations our impression, and our impressiveness, but we are still not there to enjoy their hoped-for admiration of our achievements. In another illustration of such "castles," London, my home city, is a city that is particularly well covered with statues of great men and women of the past. You can hardly turn a corner without encountering some king or queen, Boadicea or Cromwell, and it is surely a crowning ambition of many a person to end up so memorialized for future generations. And yet they are still dead, and I have often observed pigeons sitting happily on the heads of these once-great tyrants and deputies, Nelsons and commanders, and only sometimes can I resist an inner smile at the effrontery of what pigeons do, not only in the presence of but also on the shoulders of Queen Victoria, for instance.

For most of us, our hope to be remembered after we are gone is tied up in our family, and so Jesus' call to follow him beyond and above that—"Let the dead bury their own dead"—is suitably radical and unnerving. But it is also the solution to boredom; it is even more the way to life.

In the second of Jesus' seven "I Am" statements in John's Gospel, we find Jesus saying, "I am the light of the world" (John 8:12). This is a characteristic turn of phrase for Jesus in John's Gospel, reverberating back to John's famous prologue (John 1:1-18), his introduction to his Gospel, where the light comes into the world, and is not overcome by the darkness. For John, the world is defined not merely as "the place where everyone exists" but more as "the place where everyone exists as he or she chooses and doesn't do what God wants." The world, for John, and Jesus in John's Gospel, is more often not just "everyone" but "everyone in rebellion against God."

So when Jesus says earlier in John's Gospel that "God so loved the world, that he gave his only Son," the focus is not only upon the amazing love of God for all those people who live in the world. That is certainly a part of it, and a wonderful truth. But the more amazing aspect that Jesus wants us to consider is not just that God loves everyone but that God loves everyone just as they are, full of sin, darkness, and evil. This is "the world" to which Jesus is the light: "For God so loved the world, that he gave his only Son, that whoever believes in him should not perish but have eternal life." John 3:16, a verse that many people even now remember by heart, points the way to life through believing in Jesus.

With that context in mind, we come now to the second of Jesus' "I Am" statements in chapter 8 of John's Gospel and there discover that he says, "I am the light of the world." The picture is of a beam of light shining into a darkened room or upon a darkened globe. But it is more than light; it is life too. "I am the light of the world," Jesus says, "Whoever follows me will not walk in darkness, but will have the light of life."

It's easy to define these statements in quick and neat theological categories: world = sin, light = Jesus, life = eternal life/heaven. Each of those equations is 100 percent true, yet sometimes their very familiarity robs us of their meaning. Life is something we get "in the future," but it is also something that we have, if we follow Jesus, right now: it is life abundant. Of course, abundant is different from easy, but it is the kind of abundance that makes the thrill of bonds born on the front line of Afghanistan pale beside the excitement of following Jesus.

This *mysterion* of the gospel, that which was hidden but has now been revealed—ultimately in his own person—this great *life*, light, comes from following him. He is the Creator; he is the Redeemer; therefore, all that is life comes from a close connection to him. He is the "I AM," Yahweh, and in following him we walk in the light of life, the life that created all, and in Jesus the life that redeems all.

It is eternal life in the future, but that life begins in the present, in abundance, even if not in ease and sloth. It is exciting, it is thrilling, and it introduces us to the family bond of others, who are on the front line with Jesus following him—letting the dead bury their own dead.

Dead End

Not only are we bored, some of us; we feel that life has come to a dead end, that there are no more hills to take, or adventures to have, or mountain ranges to discover. This sense of ennui is not simply an individual matter but a reflection of a broader feeling throughout our culture today.

Much recent Christian rhetoric has been one great long attempt to prevent, if not undo, the changes that took place in the 1960s and '70s. The so-called permissive society— where sexual experimentation was normalized, where barriers between various social groupings were attempted to be destroyed, and where traditional religion was lampooned—was by no means all bad, but it led some into disastrous quagmires. Of course, there were real gains and freedom for others, but those decades also washed up many souls on the shores of breakdown, and as people grew older, they began to look for firmer ground on which to stand.

And so, time and time again, we hear from our pulpits, and in our books, in various ways that we need to learn again to submit, to obey, to follow the rules, to be good family people, to hold on to traditional ways of looking at life. As understandable as such an emphasis is, when presented without subtlety it can fail to give the right impression that true authority actually sets us free. As Christian ethicist Oliver O'Donovan has argued, we cannot sensibly ask ourselves whether we shall have an authority or not; we simply "stumble upon it."[1] For while wrong authority is a great evil, true authority is a description of reality to which we must submit or suffer the consequences. Gravity, for instance, is a form of authority invested in reality: you can jump off a high building if you like, but the authority of gravity will bring you back down to earth with a bump (or a death). Authority, true authority, is not something imposed on us from outside, against the facts of life as they are, but an expression of reality: if you go under water for long enough, you will die (the authority of oxygen); if you go into outer space without a spacesuit, you will die (the authority of space); if you do not drink water, you will die (the authority of water); and if you do not follow Jesus, you will also die (the authority of God). God's authority is not imposed on us from above, in the sense of different from reality; it is a description of what is, for he is the Creator, and we are his creatures.

That is why God says, "Seek me and live" (Amos 5:4), for in seeking God we find life, and in following Jesus we find life, as the means to life, as Life himself, as the "I Am" who is the "light of life." There is authority—enormous authority—in Jesus saying, "Leave the dead to bury their own dead." And this must be preached, and believed, for it is what is.

Today we remain a "permissive society" rebelling against authority, like a man jumping off a high building rebelling against gravity for the sheer thrill of it. Now, however, there is also a different, and darker, evil that many of us feel and struggle to give name to, making us precisely the reverse of a permissive society: a terrorized society.

We can see this in growing rates of crime and increased numbers of petty dictators with world-destroying arsenals of weapons. Now, because creation groans with the misuse to which it has been submitted, governments the world over are asserting more and more "authority" in an attempt to stem the tide. These things are cyclical. A generation older than mine in England can remember a time when it was not just rare to see a beggar on the streets, but they had literally never seen one. Now they are two a penny, some malicious no doubt, others incredibly needy, some mentally disturbed, still others the victims of family breakdown. Even longer ago, in England, if Charles Dickens's descriptions of Victorian London are to be believed, the suffering, horror, and shame of the underclass were far worse than anything any of us today have ever seen, outside of a particularly poor region of a developing country.

These things change depending on the basic morality of the situation. With a society that is predominantly "me centered," the big society of people caring for one another, of families stable together, and of citizens looking out for one another tends to disappear. What is government to do when basic morality frays? Inevitably, as history time and again shows, what it does is it rolls up its sleeves and asserts more authority. This is inevitable and at times good, but it has a darker underside, as we increasingly feel the pressure of control, of a "big brother" society, of identity theft, and of decisions taken by powerful bureaucracies with which we have very little involvement.

In this way, Jesus' command to follow him and let the dead bury their own dead is about as radical, countercultural, and compelling as it comes. He is not simply asserting his authority; he is freeing us from evil authority. If Jesus' authority is so great that a proper human activity is trumped by his call to follow him, then what of evil authority, what of the dehumanizing authority of bureaucracies gone mad, of corporations controlling our destinies? In Jesus' day, the great power that carried this feeling was the power of Rome, and it is noteworthy that Jesus famously tells us to give what is due to Caesar, and that Paul tells even the Romans to submit to the proper authorities. Jesus is no political revolutionary, in the sense of someone who takes up arms and urges his followers to set up a new state on better lines: his kingdom is not of this world.

But his authority is above this world too, and he calls us to live by the terms of that other world even within this world. And it is that which gives life, and stops us feeling that we have reached a dead end, as individuals, and as a society.

WORK

Perhaps the most obvious way that this need to live life to the full comes to all of us is in the daily grind of the working week, whether that work happens in the home or outside of the home, whether we are trading stocks, mending teeth, getting up in the middle of the night to feed babies, or studying for exams. Work is a great leveler. Work is run through with its own hierarchies and power issues, of course, but work, the necessity for work in most of our normal lives, says something about who we are as people, as well as something about what is wrong. Work is created good; we are gardeners, all of us, with soil to till, trees to tend, and vegetables to grow, whether literally or figuratively. We are made for such labor, and it can be sweet to us, the thrill of achievement, the joy of the chase, the satisfaction of completion. But at the same time work is surrounded by, and infested with, thorns because we live in a world that is outside of the garden of Eden, where work has become the labor that produces sweat and frustration, where the ground grows thorns.

I remember when I was an undergraduate student at Cambridge looking for summer jobs. I went to the usual employment centers, assuming that with a college degree under way, finding a temporary summer job would not be at all hard. How wrong I was! I rapidly discovered that I was trained to do almost nothing. As we went through the list of potential temporary employment options, I rapidly ran out of any avenues to pursue, until at last I found my expertise in washing up dishes. For many a summer, as a young man, I would find myself in the kitchen at the back of some massive corporate café, arms deep in soap suds, scrubbing away at enormous pots and pans, while thinking about Nietzsche, Kierkegaard, Whiggish interpretations of history, and Marxist views of capitalism and Christianity.

> Work can tell us who we are—but it also tells who we are not.

At one location, each time I successfully cleaned another industrial-sized pot or pan and left it gleaming on the tray beside the sink, someone who was employed further up the hierarchy than me would inevitably come up and congratulate me. "Well done," the person would say without fail. "That's clean." The first commendation surprised me; when I noticed that it happened without fail, it bemused me. What did they expect? It not to be clean? How hard could it be to clean these pans? They were not praising me even for doing it fast, just doing it. It took me some while to put two and two together because at least half, if not more, of my mind was still engaged in endless intellectual pursuits. I eventually inquired about the person who usually did my job, and in whose place I was temporarily standing. I felt as though I was being treated as if I were mentally deficient, and I found that the man who normally stood there cleaning pans was, in fact, mentally deficient. They were kind; they were generous; they assumed that because I was cleaning pots and pans for a living, I must also be mentally deficient. How my Cambridge pride reared up! And how good it was for me.

Work is a great leveler, especially good, gritty, hard work, without any frills or pretenses. Augustine, after he was grabbed and made a priest and later a bishop by the canny citizens of Hippo and employed as coadjutor with the previous incumbent, would reflect on the great privilege of gardening. He saw that simple pastime as benefiting the human soul immensely. Some work is far more grandiose and appeals so much to our vanity or our desires to make a difference in the world that it is too easy for us to fulfill the old dictum of worshiping our work, working at our play, and playing at our worship.

Work can do us good. Hard work can keep us out of mischief and help us avoid the idle hands that they say are the devil's tools. Work can be done for the Lord, as the Bible teaches; in fact, work should be done for the Lord. It is part of our Christian responsibility, our joy, and our orientation as Christians to believe that the earth is the Lord's and all there is in it. God made us to take care of the garden. As created beings, Christians or not, we have creativity to express his divine handiwork in us and in the world. Work can vibrate with meaning; it can tell us who we are, but it also tells who we are not.

There are the thorns. Because work is not saving, it is not ultimately satisfying. It is intended to be a form of worship, but it is not intended to be worshiped. Work is not life, and life is more than work; we are not meant to live to work, any more than we are meant to work to live. We live to walk with Jesus and find life, abundant life, in him.

If only we could find the thrill again of who Jesus is and what he can do with us and through us, our working lives would take on a new meaning and point to a higher and deeper worship beyond merely labor and human achievement. It is something like this that must have struck the official who came to Jesus for help (John 4:46-54) and received the second of seven of Jesus' signs of who he is in John's Gospel.

The official was a powerful man, perhaps a significant administrator of King Herod himself. He may have been of the royal family or connected to the ruling aristocracy at the time. But he had discovered how limited was that power. For despite his authority over others, his political influence mattered not one bit when his own son was ill and about to die.

He had experienced not just the thorns in his work, but the thorns in his life. How ironic it is to have such power in your professional world, and at the same time to be so helpless over the life of the one you love. He had come to Jesus for help, hearing perhaps of the sign he had performed already at Cana in Galilee. Jesus at first seems to keep at a distance, saying, "Unless you see signs and wonders you will not believe."

Does Jesus have no compassion? In a moment Jesus will miraculously heal the official's son, but it is instructive to realize that these are *signs*, not healings, as described in John's Gospel. The official has asked Jesus to heal his son because the son was at the point of death, and Jesus' response not only is standoffish but also points to something else: faith. For Jesus the point is not the healing itself; instead, it is the sign of a greater healing of which the recovery of the official's son will speak: the relationship, the "life" now and forever, that comes through faith in who Jesus is.

John tells us that that is the significance of all the signs: to give us faith in Jesus and therefore life in his name. Later in his

Gospel, John tells us: "Now Jesus did many other signs in the presence of the disciples, which are not written in this book; but these are written so that you may believe that Jesus is the Christ, the Son of God, and that by believing you may have life in his name" (John 20:30-31).

That's what actually happened to the official himself. As he found that his son had been healed, he inquired when it had taken place. When he discovered it was at the same time as when Jesus had said, "Your son will live," then, "he himself believed, and all his household." This successful working man, with his entire household, found life in Jesus' name above and beyond his official position and the desperate need of his son that his professional expertise could not fix.

For an ancient official, in many ways the master of life and death, or certainly the purveyor of authority to dispense and take away life, to come to Jesus to solve the problem of life and imminent death was indeed a great sign. These signs, like Moses' signs before Pharaoh, function as a way of saying that God through Jesus is doing a great deliverance, a second and bigger and better Exodus. Not the Nile turned to blood, but water turned to wine. Not staffs becoming snakes, but people coming back to life. Not the pagan nation's children dying, but the official's child being brought back to life through this great salvation—this life—that Jesus is bringing.

CHURCH

Work can seem like the opposite of an exciting life, and for many of us today, our church experience can seem similarly disappointing. We know it is necessary, or worthy, or helpful in some shape or form, no doubt. But for many people, and perhaps you include yourself among them (I know I have felt this way at times too), church can seem more like eating your vegetables than the fullness of life of enjoying a really good steak. Someone told me once that he knew that coming to church regularly was important, just like going to a gym was important; it kept you spiritually fit, and without it you were less likely to be so spiritually healthy. That attitude tells me that although church is still thought of as worthy, it is no longer thought of as necessary, much less exciting. I do not *have* to go to a gym; I can if I want, and I know it is good for me. It costs me something, and it is not (for most people) an entirely pleasant experience. But there it is. If I want to lose a few pounds in the wrong places, and gain some muscle in the right places, then I need to go to the gym. I'll pay my dues (or my tithe); I'll turn up regularly for a while, and then forget it for a while. Sometimes I'll just take a break from church—or the gym—because any kind of routine can get stale, and I need to freshen things up by going to a different club, or taking a run outside, or just relaxing in front of a good movie, or reading a worthy book, or surfing the Internet a little bit by myself at home.

This, of course, is very different from the biblical attitude toward church, where church is seen as a body and as a bride; that is, as intrinsically and organically connected. It's more like a family than a club. As a member of the body, you are connected, and when we meet together, we express that necessary connection, which exists whether we like it or not, and cannot be removed, any more than the eye can say to the foot that it does not need it. No bride excited and ready for the great day walks down the aisle with the attitude of "Well, I suppose I'll have to go through this because it is good for me." There is a relationship that we have with Christ, as his bride, as his body, which we experience and have organically, as well as organizationally, together.

It is no accident that as church life and commitment have moved toward the membership of a gym in many people's minds, our sense of community life and excitement has diminished similarly. Without church, the community of God in the city of God, we are left more as isolated individuals, bouncing off one another with no real interaction, no more than a brief glance in a sweaty haze at a gym or a furtive smile in a checkout line at a store. "We" in a very real sense do not exist; it is now simply a collection of "I."

> **Submission is not slavery; submission is love.**

Human beings are not made for such isolation. If the Bible is true, we are made in God's image, and God is essentially a social being. God is not an isolated unit, forever satisfied as an individualistic "I," but is a trinity, a social network of love in his own heart and mind, constantly communicating and loving and knowing and being together. And a deep part of that image that he has given to us is expressed in our need for relationship with him, and with one another. *Need* is too mild a word; I need food, I need shelter, I need drink. Rarely would someone say that he or she "needs" an arm or "needs" eyes. We do not just need each other, and we do not just need God. We cannot live without God, in any real sense; and in any real sense we, as a singular "I," cannot live without being members of the body of Christ jointly.

This does not mean that my basic individuality is lost in a smush of grayness; we have all the rainbow colors of difference, heightened even more, and only made possible, by the light and life of God. Unlike in some philosophies of life, Christians do believe that we have an actual, real "I." There is someone called "me," and each "I" is of great value, divine worth, made in God's image. "I" have responsibility; "I" make choices.

But our view of life is not reflected in the polytheism of the many gods of hill and stream, of wood and dell, of pagan mythologies, where in some circumstances "I" disappears in value before the need of the community. Nor is our view of the "I" formed by those philosophies of life that so lift up the "I," or the "superego," that community needs are lost in the will to power. Instead, we believe that we are made, all of us as individual "I"s in the presence of and in the image of God himself. The Trinity, with its relationship of one and the many, with its submissive authority structure where the Son submits to the Father without being any less than the divine Son and where the Spirit proceeds from the Father and the Son—this structure of reality means that life is not just a solo experience.

In all likelihood our loneliness as people in this very individual age is due to our misunderstanding of that most controversial word these days: *submission*. Without submission I cannot have friendship at all, and without submission to authority I cannot have community or society, let alone church. Submission is not slavery; submission is love, as the Trinity proves, and as every Christian shows who sits under God's word on Sundays in church, the word of life.

ADVENTURE

This longing for the life that is large, the life that is living, is seen no more clearly than in what is called the entertainment industry. What does it say about our need to find the life that is living, and how desperate we are for it that we will watch television for countless hours, seeing thousands of nameless couples in intimate relationships, doing what previous generations only imagined and never saw enacted, as our entertainment? What does it mean for our time and our day when we have seen, by a very young age these days, disfigured faces, heads lopped off shoulders with blood pouring out, dismembered bodies, bodies disemboweled and dehumanized all for our entertainment?

It is interesting to watch, occasionally, some of the older films of previous generations and compare what was thought to be risqué then with what is thought to be risqué now. An Alfred Hitchcock movie, one of the scary ones, is relatively tame by comparison to even some PG-13s, let alone an R-rated movie. These movements forward (or backward) are not to be ignored, because what they mean is that we are socially becoming more used to extreme forms of entertainment, without noticing that it is gradually getting not just more extreme, but positively perverse. All in the name of adventure, excitement, entertainment.

The most exciting, dangerous, adventurous year of my life

was spent on what was a new frontier, in a republic that had only just come out of civil war and was still controlled by young men on the streets with machine guns and by local mafia bosses with their little militias. I don't remember watching TV once that whole year, but I certainly remember my heart pounding most days, and fear catching my throat in the middle of the night. I had no need to seek adventure secondhand; I was living all the adventure and more that I could handle almost every day, sometimes every minute of every day.

It is the safe people who populate the seats in the Coliseum and observe the games from a safe distance and watch the blood on the sand for entertainment. Our society has found ways to make it look as if people are dying for our pleasure on a small (or big) screen when really the death, the dismemberment, the intimacy of passion, is merely being enacted. We may not watch people who are literally killing each other for our pleasure, but if we watch people who are performing intimate acts for our pleasure, how much more sophisticated are we than the decadent years of the late Roman Empire? And who will be the barbarians at the gates of our late Western civilization?

We (both "I" and "We") are in need of finding life again, revitalization, as perhaps few societies have been. We are skipping along the edge of a precipice: economy in tatters at times, the rich getting richer and less publicly generous than in previous generations, the big society less obviously one in which we all get a chance to live, and morals decaying at a rate that a generation before could have hardly believed.

Risk

Our craving for secondhand adventure, surrogate adventure, is a "sign" of an appetite that has gotten used to tastes of an extreme and relatively spicy kind. Pornography is one example. In our current lack of life that we get to live in reality, we're bored. So we need to escape into a life of fantasy. Vegas is another example: gambling, the great pull of risk.

In a sense, it is nothing new. These escapes have always existed in human society, games of chance that have caught the unwary and robbed the children and spouses of those unwary. Charles Dickens tells in *The Old Curiosity Shop* of a man caught in this kind of trap and destroyed by an individual seeking to make as much profit as possible from this man's gambling debts. Las Vegas is not a new thing; it is just an old thing in a new place, but the popularity of such games of chance, of the lottery, of the extremely unlikely chance of ever winning such fortunes, and the great damage they often do even if they are won, tell us something about the sort of life that we do not have, and somehow still long for inside. Those without life abundant look for life in titillation or in risk. Often these bits of entertainment are not just addictive but a "sign" of a need for a real life that is healthy and that lasts forever.

Perhaps nowhere is this kind of thrill shown more clearly than in the second of seven of the letters to the churches of the Roman province of Asia in John's Revelation. Unlike all the other churches, except also Philadelphia, Smyrna has no rebuke coming from the lips of the Lord Jesus: it is a faithful,

good church, and he does not tell it off in the slightest, but
encourages it and commends it:

> And to the angel of the church in Smyrna write: "The
> words of the first and the last, who died and came to
> life. I know your tribulation and your poverty (but you
> are rich) and the slander of those who say that they are
> Jews and are not, but are a synagogue of Satan. Do not
> fear what you are about to suffer. Behold, the devil is
> about to throw some of you into prison, that you may
> be tested, and for ten days you will have tribulation.
> Be faithful unto death, and I will give you the crown
> of life. He who has an ear, let him hear what the Spirit
> says to the churches. The one who conquers will not
> be hurt by the second death." (Revelation 2:8-11)

Jesus gives the church at Smyrna no criticism or condem-
nation, but he does give it a serious challenge! "Be faithful
unto death." They are about to suffer in a serious and extreme
form. For some reason, those who oppose the fledging Christian movement are about to fling, under the direction of Satan
himself (though they may not even know it), some of these
new Christians into jail for their faith. Coming out of a Jewish
movement, as a messianic proclamation that Jesus is the king
of the Jews, they have long been protected by the status that
the traditional Jewish religion was given in the Roman Empire.
But they are soon going to be finally distinguished from this
religion that is turning its back upon Jesus, and so they will
move out of their protection and become vulnerable to persecution. Depending on the exact date of Revelation, such

persecutions may have been centrally sanctioned by Rome or local outbursts of pogroms against the new Christians.

Whatever the precise historical background, however, the spiritual dynamic was clear, and Jesus tells the Smyrnan church that they need to be ready to be "faithful to death."

That's certainly a risk, and it is certainly an adventure. It puts bungee jumping off the Eiffel Tower into the shade. There is no safety here. It is a firefight that is coming, and there is real potential that in the battle, some will literally die. It's a strange place to finish a chapter on "life," and it is strange to our ears to realize that Jesus does not promise to rescue them from this "first death." Some of them *will* die. They need to be faithful right up until then.

One of the reasons why so much of our Christian faith feels limp is because we are not called upon to be faithful to death. There is no risk. And because there is no risk, there is little adventure. But it is only

> There's no need for life by entertainment, life by surrogate, when we are living on the high-end adrenaline of following Jesus.

as we take the risk of standing up for the unpopular virtues and causes and beliefs against which our culture today rages but which are key and core to biblical Christian faith, it is only then as we face "death" by a thousand cuts of criticism and seek to be faithful right to the end, that we can hear the promise given to the church at Smyrna: "Be faithful unto death, and I will give you the crown of life"—the crown of life, life abundantly now, life forever, which begins here and is about following Jesus, the light of life, which goes through the grave to resurrection and eternity and immortality.

There's no need for "Second Life," life by entertainment, life by surrogate, when we are living on the high-end adrenaline—in the middle of the dishes, the desk, the work, the worship of God—of following Jesus, even to death, and from there to life.

A Day for Truth

As Jesus passed on from there, he saw a man called Matthew
sitting at the tax booth, and he said to him, "Follow me."
And he rose and followed him.

—Matthew 9:9

Given that Peter Hitchens was the brother of Christopher Hitchens—the renowned atheist—his book *The Rage Against God*, articulating Peter's traditional faith in the Jesus of the Bible, is surprising. They grew up in a home that did not force religion upon the children, went to a school where Anglican Christian faith was a norm, and both rebelled against traditional Christian faith. Peter recounts a story of a ceremonial burning of a Bible to indicate his newfound liberty (a burning that, he whimsically tells us, was not so exciting, because Bibles do not burn as well as he had hoped).

The two brothers debated publicly before Christopher died, though Peter seems to have had enough of such attempts to create a potential carnival out of the brothers' differences.

While they strongly disagreed, they agreed on at least the importance of telling the truth in as plain English as possible, whatever the cost.

Telling the truth is an art form that we have come to despise, or at least have suspicions about the possibility of achieving. Peter Hitchens gives his take on the cultural and psychological reasons for why many of his generation of Englishmen have rebelled against their Christian faith, naming, for him, the two world wars, and the church's capitulation to the governing class in those world wars, as powerful reasons for many people giving up on their faith. He dispenses with the traditional atheist views fairly briefly, once the story of his own return to the faith is told, especially taking time to explain how religions are not the cause of all the wars in the world.

Many people still seem to think that the Crusades were mainly about religion, that the wars and violence in Northern Ireland were the church's fault—when in fact Peter Hitchens is surely right that what such conflicts actually teach us is that we are at war with one another and will use whatever powerful tools we can find to gain the advantage. It is a doctrine of humanity that mirrors the Christian view of us being in the image of God and yet fallen. It is also worth saying that some of the bloodiest conflicts and most notorious crimes have been committed by atheistic regimes, and it is certainly true that anyone who saw the effects of atheistic communism on normal people cannot ever want to go there again.

Yet seeing two brothers sparring against each other, while it may even the odds for Christians being the target of intellectual snobbery from elite academic atheists, does not itself establish "the truth" one way or another; in fact, you might say it is evidence that finding the truth is as hard as it ever was. If two brothers, equally bright, equally articulate, growing up in a similar environment, can end up with two such different opinions, what are the grounds for discovering what is the truth about this matter of ultimate importance? Perhaps the very different personalities that Peter and Christopher Hitchens seem to have had almost from birth is as good an explanation for their different viewpoints as anything else. We may not be coming any closer to the truth but instead merely observing two brothers not getting along that well and certainly not agreeing about God.

Atheist Richard Dawkins's work does not take us much further, though as a scientist he makes great claims to objectivity. But those who have lived among or moved among academic scientists will know that you are just as likely to find Bible-believing Christians who are scientists as you are to find Bible-believing Christians who are historians. In fact, rather more likely, for at least the scientific disciplines encourage people to make up their minds based on the evidence rather than to generate neat, persuasive essays arguing one side (or the other) of the case. For every Dawkins who is controversial, you have a John Polkinghorne, a Cambridge professor of theoretical physics, who argues the opposite case; for every Christopher Hitchens you have a Peter Hitchens; and there are also the Alister McGraths, the John Lennoxes, and so on, claiming scientific compatibility with their Christian faith.

So when we come to a well-known statement like Jesus' that "the truth will set you free," we would be forgiven for thinking that knowing the truth is a fine ideal, and may indeed give the promised result of genuine freedom, but that truth itself as the Truth is unattainable.

This is why Jesus' third of the seven "Follow me" statements of Matthew's Gospel is particularly helpful, because Jesus does not argue about Matthew's tax collecting but commands Matthew to follow him. This call has the same sense of unembarrassed authority with regard to what the right or true thing is to do or believe as Jesus' famous saying about the truth setting you free. In full context, Jesus says that the truth comes from abiding (or remaining) in, trusting in, believing in, or listening to his word: "If you abide in my word, you are truly my disciples, and you will know the truth, and the truth will set you free" (John 8:31-32).

This is a helpful comparison to what Jesus says to Matthew because, while John's Gospel has a different audience in mind and a distinctive style, the underlying issue in Matthew's call is related. After Matthew follows Jesus, we are told about a party with Jesus and many tax collectors "and sinners." Remember how hated tax collectors were in the ancient world because they were given a license, in effect, to lie and cheat as part of collecting taxes for the foreign occupying force of the Roman Empire. It is not just that they were symbolic agents of Rome but also that they were "on the make"; they collected more than was necessary to line their own pockets. Going to a tax collector was like going to

> When people reject God, or the truth about God, what they often reject is the "God" that Jesus rejected too.

a corrupt garage mechanic and being told that your car needs this, that, and the other when really an oil change would do. Truth was definitely lacking from the traditional tax collector repertoire, as was righteousness.

So Jesus is criticized for eating with such people, for soiling his hands with cheats and thieves. No one would be as unpopular today, other than perhaps a politician who had been proved to have lied on the campaign trail and embezzled funds for his own enrichment. Jesus was with "sinners," people who were socially despised. People who were not known for telling the truth.

But what *was* the truth of the matter? What was the truth about God in regard to such people? Were the Pharisees on the side of truth when they distanced themselves from the immoral? Surely God is a holy God, and so Jesus certainly should not be participating publicly with people who were known to have been involved as collaborators in the equivalent of the Vichy regime? But Jesus' "truth" is *the* Truth, and is quite different from what the religion of the Pharisees would have expected: "Those who are well have no need of a physician, but those who are sick. Go and learn what this means: 'I desire mercy, and not sacrifice.' For I came not to call the righteous, but sinners" (Matthew 9:12-13).

MODERN LIES

This is the most radical moral teaching of any religious leader ever, though also traditional because Jesus was rightly interpreting the Old Testament, from which he was quoting.

What Jesus said, in effect, is that the big lie behind the Pharisees' objection to his behavior is a wrong view of God. They needed to meet his God, who desires mercy, not sacrifice.

The same untruth is behind many modern lies, because when people reject God, or the truth about God, what they often reject is the "God" that Jesus rejected too. Like a good philosopher, Jesus says that in the search for the truth about God, the most important place to start is with making sure we have our definitions right: what sort of God are we talking about? The "God" many people reject is the God of the Pharisees, who desires sacrifice, not mercy.

In the movie *A Few Good Men*, there is a well-known, unforgettable courtroom scene. Tom Cruise plays a lawyer, Lieutenant Daniel Kaffee, who has to cross-examine perhaps the most intimidating man ever, Colonel Nathan R. Jessup, portrayed by Jack Nicholson. Jessup runs a hard outfit, and under his command he has created an atmosphere of intimidation that finally, with his permission and command, led to the murder of a young marine. Kaffee, at last, confronts Jessup in court and demands, "I want the truth," to which Jessup memorably bawls back, "You can't handle the truth!"

Kaffee insists all the more that he wants to hear the truth, and Jessup in the end gives way and unfolds the whole story boldly in front of the entire court. Yes, he had given the order that had led to the marine's death, and he was not ashamed of it. It was people like Kaffee, who lived a long way away from Guantanamo Bay, who did not understand the kind of compromises that had to be made to ensure that they could sleep easily at night. Meanwhile, men like Colonel Jessup—hard men, determined men, aggressive men—kept the peace on the frontier and prevented disaster from happening to everyone else. For Jessup, the marine's death was, in the end, a necessary crime, collateral damage, not pleasant, but when men do such things in the name of a greater good, then society itself is protected against a worse evil.

The truth that Kaffee is not meant to be able to handle is, then, not just the truth of what happened to the poor unfortunate marine; the truth is that such things—in Colonel Jessup's mind—are necessary for Kaffee and others like him to live the kind of life that he has grown used to living: a safe life, a prosperous life, an innocent life. But without blood it could not happen.

This fairly well-known Hollywood movie moment illustrates how sometimes we do not know the truth because we are not able or willing to deal with it, to "handle" it. Or at least that is why some people try to protect us from the truth. There are plenty of examples of this in normal, everyday life. For instance, if you have cancer, sometimes you have to fight a little ("I want the truth!") to find out what the doctors really think are your chances of survival, particularly if they feel that you are especially vulnerable, whether you are older or younger or in a fragile state of mind ("You can't handle the truth").

There are occasions, no doubt, to withhold total disclosure, and if we went around all the time telling everyone not just the truth, but the whole truth, we would hear more detail than we wanted from all our friends about their boils and bowel movements and every inner wave of emotion or thought, however trivial. There are reasons to withhold the truth for a season, such as when, in high school, an educational program tells you that a particular element of physics is certain, but then you study the same subject at a university and find that it is rather less certain than you were first told.

But there are many truths about life that are rather more difficult for us to handle—like the truth that we will all die. We all "know" this truth, somewhere deep down, but the truth is frequently hidden from us. In fact, much of modern life seems to tell us that there is always plenty of time, time to entertain yourself, and that if you work hard at it, you can stay young, fit, and beautiful. When we bring this "truth" out into the open, the truth that is sold to us by many a facial cream, or gym, we realize that it is ridiculous, but we rarely talk about it because we "can't handle it," or at least not very often.

But death is the question that life must answer, the truth it must discover. If that truth is not discovered, then no other question matters. The riddle, if remaining unraveled, renders all else meaningless. Atheists will tell us that the answer is simple; as Bertrand Russell put it, "I believe that when I die I shall rot." But for many of us the truth of the matter is far from being so easy: we feel the absence of a loved one; when we stare at a cadaver, we do not sense that the person is "there" anymore; death does not appear to us to be natural but a great evil to be fought against or pushed through to the ultimate good beyond. The truth is that people do not easily believe that when they die, they rot any more than people easily believe that when they jump off a tall building, they fly, or that if they apply the right facial cream, they will remove all wrinkles. These so-called truths have to be marketed to us; we are not easily persuaded.

In reality, most people naturally end up thinking that there is some life beyond, that there is indeed a Great Reckoning to which we will all give an account.

That does not make that truth true, just because people naturally believe it, but it does mean that the modern attempt to sweep the truth under the carpet by various means and techniques, and not face up to our own death, and answer that riddle, is a terrible lie.

Big-Picture God

But we tend to believe that lie, or avoid the truth that we find hard to handle, because the alternative is to have to face up to a God, of some sort at least, and that God is often in our minds the God of sacrifice, not of mercy. We run from him, we disobey him, we despise him, not because he is worth running from or worth despising or unworthy of obedience but because this "God" in our minds is distorted. Sin is having the wrong idea of God and acting upon it: you can see this in the original sin, which became the model for all other sins. Adam and Eve ate the apple, not just because the apple was pleasing, but because more importantly they came to believe that God was the kind of God who would stop them from having pleasure. He was against them, not for them; he was the divine spoilsport, the God of sacrifice, not mercy.

Obviously, in some sense, God does require sacrifice, which is what makes Jesus' statement (and the quotation from the Old Testament) so interesting. God set up a system where countless animals were sacrificed to take away

sin, all pointing to the fulfillment of that Old Testament sac-
rificial system, the Lamb of God, who takes away the sin of
the world. God, therefore, must in some way desire sacrifice
because he ordered that sacrifices be performed and because
Jesus is the sacrifice who removes our sin. So what does Jesus
mean that God desires mercy and not sacrifice? He is quoting from the prophet Hosea, who preached that God's people
had abandoned "mercy," that is, *hesed*, God's covenant love,
and instead attempted to cover the need for mercy by participating in corrupt and vain sacrifices (Hosea 6:6). They were
like people who robbed and committed adultery; who did
not care for the poor; who even worshiped false gods in their
heart; but kept on "going through the motions" and doing
"sacrifices" as a safety-net approach to religion.

This is not only what *they* did; it is something the Pharisees did; it is something *we* typically do. We tend to end up not
trusting God, the real God of the Bible, not acting in mercy
toward those around us, because we have made God to be a
"religious" God, who enjoys a big religious celebration, rather
than the God whom Jesus represents, the God whose sacrifice
for us is mercy toward us. Sacrifice without mercy is not biblical sacrifice; it is just vain ceremony. Instead, the mercy of God
is why Jesus sacrificed himself for us, and why we are called
upon to act in mercy toward others as well.

This Big Picture of Who God Is cannot be better summarized than in Jesus' seven "I Am" sayings in John's Gospel. We
need to understand and believe who God is by way of understanding and believing who Jesus is. Richard Bauckham studied these seven "I Am" sayings in John's Gospel and believes

that they reflect the seven "I AM" sayings found on the lips of God in the Old Testament, the first in Deuteronomy, the other six between Isaiah 40 and Isaiah 55. The third of these seven "I Am" sayings comes in Isaiah 43:10-11:

> "You are my witnesses," declares the LORD,
>   "and my servant whom I have chosen,
> that you may know and believe me
>   and understand that I am he.
> Before me no god was formed,
>   nor shall there be any after me.
> I, I am the LORD,
>   and besides me there is no savior."

God is declaring himself and reaching out to his people, so that they should know him and understand who he is, that he is the I AM, that there is no other true God, for he is the Lord, and besides him there is no savior. God reveals himself as a God who acts in mercy, in covenant *hesed* love, in saving action, on behalf of his people, and it is this that will reveal who he is.

And so, the third of seven of Jesus' "I Am" statements in John's Gospel is a word picture: Jesus is the door of salvation. He is the one we have to go "through" to experience God; he is the Savior, to use Isaiah's language; he is "the door" for the sheep in Jesus' depiction in John 10: "Truly, truly, I say to you, I am the door of the sheep. All who came before me are thieves and robbers, but the sheep did not listen to them. I am the door. If anyone enters by me, he will be saved and will go in and out and find pasture" (John 10:7-9). When we are called to follow Jesus, we are being called to this God, not the other "God," not

"I desire mercy, and not sacrifice. For I came not to call the righteous, but sinners."

the God who we think desires sacrifice, not mercy, but the God who is mercy, who is saving, who is the door for the sheep.

Of course, all these "sevens" are not parallel in some mathematical game that is hidden and that we have to discover. They show us that God is concerned with providing us the key aspects of who he is, the truth about who he is as we are considering this Wednesday.

Imagine with me that you are Matthew, probably also called Levi (Luke 5:27), the son of Alphaeus (Mark 2:14). You are in the pay of Herod Antipas, who in turn reports to Rome, and you are occupying a tax booth bordering the Sea of Galilee at Capernaum, taxing fishermen for Herod, in turn for Rome. Later you follow Jesus, and in time will become the author of what we know as "Matthew's Gospel." But for now you are a tax collector. You are hated, feared, reviled. Simon (later called Peter) and Andrew are likely to be with Jesus too, for they have already said yes to following Jesus.

Perhaps you recognize Simon and Andrew because, after all, they were fisherman in the Sea of Galilee, and this is your "patch," your area of tax collecting. Does a snarl come out of their lips, quickly bitten back, unsure now what the appropriate response is for followers of this Rabbi Jesus? Does a glimmer of avarice appear in your eyes or fear that you will have to confront them and try to take from them the taxes that they will surely not want to pay? What is the truth of the matter in this encounter? Your other name, "Levi," perhaps indicates some connection to the tribe of Levi, from which the priests came, and you are there not serving God as such, but serving Rome, through Herod Antipas, hated usurpers, making money in an underhand way, serving money. How will Jesus approach this moment of potential conflict? Will he keep on going and avoid you? Will he despise you? Will he murmur with others about you and your hated trade?

Instead, he says, "Follow me," and with that divine authority ringing in your ears, you get up and follow him, have a feast made for Jesus (Luke 5:29), and then hear the explanation of the kind of God who Jesus is ("I Am"), the One who reaches out and saves, who has mercy: "I desire mercy, and not sacrifice. For I came not to call the righteous, but sinners."

BIG-PICTURE BIBLE

Of course, if this picture of "mercy" is taken out of its context from the rest of the Bible, it would be easy to end up with a picture of a God who is distorted, weak, pathetic. We might be able to say with Voltaire, "Of course God forgives; that's his business." But while one very common view (lie) of God today is as a Pharisaic God, not interested in the broken or the needy or the sinful, another is the view of God as so weak and puny that his forgiveness is not worth much.

It is this view of God that so repelled Nietzsche, who felt that Christianity was the "sickness," the "weakness," the "illness" of Western society and needed to be rejected because it tended to make people and society weak. What we are dealing with here, in these two rather opposite but mistaken views of God, is really a tension and a misunderstanding of the interplay between the Old and New Testaments. People have often felt that they like the God of the New Testament but not the one of the Old Testament, meaning that they found the brutal invasion of the Promised Land to be beyond acceptance in a more tolerant society, but Jesus "meek and mild" was more appealing. For Nietzsche, it may have perhaps been the other way around, that a god of the Valkyries, of warfare and deciding who will die in battle as in the old Norse legends, was somehow more attractive, because it had a toughness, a grit, a strength to it, that the Christianity he rejected did not.

This confusion between the Old and the New Testament is nothing new; it is one of the great difficulties in thinking rightly about the Christian faith, because Christianity ("Messiah-anity") is a claim that Jesus is the fulfillment of the Old Testament promises that God would rescue his people, and that this rescue, this "salvation," would go to the ends of the earth, to all nations. So right at the heart of the truth of the Christian faith is this connection between what we call the Old Testament and what we call the New Testament. It is very far from a simple problem to solve because, on the one hand, the Old Testament writings were the Scriptures of the very early church—that was their "Bible." When we read the New Testament, we find that the New Testament authors are constantly quoting from, making references to, and arguing with the Jewish religious leaders of their day about the Old Testament and how it is to be interpreted. Since then things have not become any easier.

You could make the case that most differences in belief among Christians derive from slightly different views of how the Old and the New Testament are connected. In the early centuries of the Christian church, for instance, rather creative ways of interpreting the Old Testament were used to explain a few of the more obscure passages and some of the more worrying events from a Christian point of view.

Who am I to be able to cut this Gordian knot now? To articulate a quick solution would only leave room for more creative exploration and confusion in its wake. But if we are to get to grips with the truth of Jesus, to follow the Jesus who called Matthew in truth, if we are to be able to find the truth in him and find that that truth does set us free, then we have to understand the truth about this God who desires mercy, not sacrifice. And a large part of that is seeing better the relationship between the Old Testament and the New Testament.

Of course, you can buy books and listen to sermons; that will give you simple explanations to these problems, slogans around which you can build certainty regarding the God of the whole Bible, not merely the Old Testament (or only the New Testament too, for that matter). But it is helpful to remember that Jesus himself told his disciples on the Road to Emmaus that all the Scriptures speak of him (Luke 24:27), which does not mean that we look at that with longing, that we would have heard too how Jesus put together all the texts and mourn that it does not seem so simple to us today. It means that we are given a key, a Golden Key, to unlock the treasure of the Old Testament—that it all points to Jesus, speaks about Jesus, and prepares for him.

There are also symbolic characters in the Bible that help us immensely. John the Baptist is perhaps the best in this way, because John the Baptist stands as a summary of the whole of the Old Testament. He is the last of the Old Testament figures, if you like. Where all the other prophets in the Old Testament had spoken of the Christ from a long way away, John the Baptist actually sees him with his own eyes, and when he says, "Behold, the Lamb of God, who takes away the sin of the world!" (John 1:29), John is only saying what every Scripture has said from Genesis to Malachi. But he can point to Jesus physically in front of him.

This Big Picture of the Bible gives us a Big Picture of God. It shows us that He is the God who desires mercy, not sacrifice, who came for sinners in order to save them, and that this God is not the pathetic God of Voltaire (who forgives because it is his job) or the weak God of Nietzsche. It gives us a context to the sacrifice of Jesus on the cross, which shows us who this God is when Jesus calls us to follow him again.

The unveiling of Darth Vader as the father of Luke Skywalker was a shocking revelation, a revelation most people had not thought of and were genuinely surprised by. There had been rumors perhaps, but the final idea that this evil half-machine had been Luke's father all along came as a real shock. It made us look again at the whole *Star Wars* story. "I am your father" horrified Luke and astonished us. Part of the jolt was the contrast between who Darth Vader was in our imaginations (pure evil) and who Luke Skywalker was in the story (the great savior of the Jedi); it was not like oil and water; it was like lightning and a black hole. The two do not go together.

But if instead Darth Vader had always been a rather jovial fellow, remembering Luke's birthday each year and patting him on the head affectionately at every opportunity, the revelation would have lacked storytelling punch. It would not have carried the same surprise, and it would not have been remembered as a sudden switch in the story line from the perspective of those watching. Now the whole thing seems a little trite, but at the time it was a genuine surprise.

When we hear that Jesus is friend of sinners, it cuts no ice with us because we do not have the context of the whole Bible in our minds—not that we have to remember every bit—but the Big Picture of the Bible is lacking. "Of course God forgives; that's his job." Of course Jesus died on the cross; why wouldn't he? That's the story, isn't it? That's the way it works. God is the sort of God who does that kind of thing, isn't he? God is love, and all the rest.

But this is telling the old, old story of Jesus' love without putting it in the context of the whole Bible, and therefore missing the Big Picture about God, because it misses the Big Picture about the Bible. I am not saying that in the Old Testament God is Darth Vader, and then suddenly in the New Testament he is revealed as Luke's father! That would be absurd and heretical and miss the Big Picture from yet another angle. But I *am* saying that we will not see the truth about Jesus—the one who said "Follow me" even to Matthew, the tax collector—unless we see the Big Picture of the Dark Side of the Moon and not just the paisley patterns and small-town "niceness" that we tend to think Christianity is all about.

The Old Testament helps us see this Big Picture of God.

How do we explain the origin of evil? How do we explain a God who hardens Pharaoh's heart, who loves Jacob and hates Esau? How do we explain a God who commands and disciplines his people for failing to follow this command, to wipe out the people—sometimes entirely—in the land they are invading? Each of these questions has a particular answer to it, such as the fact that the people in the land were involved in gross sin, even human sacrifice. But through it all is a view of God who is not merely "nice."

> We need a word from outside us to show us the truth of the matter, to lead us to the truth that will set us free.

And if we think this "angry" God is restricted to the Old Testament, then we need to read the New Testament a little more closely! It is Jesus who talks of hell, where the fire will not go out, where there will be weeping and gnashing of teeth. And in Revelation we see the wrath of God as so extreme that the blood flows as high as a horse's bridle for more than one and a half thousand stadia, or roughly two hundred miles. It is not that the God of the Old Testament is more wrathful than the God of the New, but that the pictures of the Old Testament are filled out in the New, and the language of the New Testament makes sense against the backdrop of the Old. This God is a God who hates sin. A God who judges. A God who chooses whom he wills—and "who are you, O man, to answer back to God [about such a choice]?" as Paul will say in his interpretation of these events in Romans 9:20.

All of this is essential to understanding a Big Picture of God from a Big Picture of the Bible, if we are to grasp the truth of what it means for Jesus to see the tax collector Matthew and say, "Follow me." If we are to see him who came for sinners, not as more and more ice cream to children who have already eaten their fill of their father's love, but as hope to the hopeless, light to those in darkness, truth to those bound up with the lie that God is the god of the Pharisees. Fear is a powerful motive, and unless we know what it is to live in the fear of eternal damnation, we will have no concept of what it means for Jesus to come and call sinners like Matthew to follow him.

BIG-PICTURE WORLD

This whole way of looking at life is so different from our society's perspective that it becomes quite difficult for us even to begin to enter into it. It's not quite the same as saying to a medieval person that the world is round (the learned then would have known that the ancients believed that the world was round), nor exactly comparable to saying that the earth goes around the sun before Galileo's views were accepted, but it is a bit like that. Certain views are instinctive to us, and we tend to gravitate to them naturally, like moths to a flame. Other views about life and God are just as true but are harder for us to hold on to as true. It is instinctive to us that a certain amount of work deserves a certain amount of pay, and it is instinctive to us that certain wrong actions deserve their "payday" as well. But the idea—the *causa gratiae*, as Augustine would call it—that God does not give us what we do deserve (mercy) but instead gives us what we do not deserve (grace) is not natural to us. By nature, we want justice (not mercy), because most of us feel that, justly speaking, we are going to be fine, that our good deeds outweigh our bad, and that while we do not precisely "deserve" to "go to heaven," we certainly do not deserve to go to hell. We assume then that we will end up in the better place at some point.

But what if actually our "natural" ideas were not always right? What if our natural view of things had been twisted in some way so that what we thought was right was actually not entirely so? And who, looking at human actions today or reading about human history or reading the Bible, could doubt that our natural instinct is sometimes quite wrong and that what we think is right can be wrong and that what we think is wrong can be right? It is not natural to think that the world is round, or that the earth goes around the sun, but such things are true. We need a word from outside us to show us what is the truth of the matter, to lead us to the truth that will set us free.

In Jesus' third of seven signs, we find just such a story about the difference between what we think, who we are, what we are capable of, and what we really need. In John 5, an invalid is trying to be healed by dipping into the pool of Bethesda, but because no one will help, and he cannot move by himself to the pool when "the water is stirred up," he has been lying there a long time. Jesus sees him. Jesus notices him; he *sees* him; the man is not just part of the crowd, he is picked out. And when the man answers Jesus' questions about why he is there, Jesus heals him—he tells him to take up his bed and walk, and the man does.

It is a great miracle, a miracle of authority and power, but it is also a sign. It is pointing to some meaning, which we are intended to grasp. It tells us that God is a compassionate God, but after all, there were many other invalids in Jerusalem at the time, so why this particular invalid? Why him? Why now? Jesus did the healing on the Sabbath, and in a wrong interpretation of the Old Testament, some of the other Jews object to this healing on a Sabbath, feeling that it is "work," when really it is compassion, perfectly legal even under the Old Testament rules. What's more, some of them object even further when they find that Jesus defends his healing on the Sabbath by saying that as God is always working, so is he, rightly discerning that by putting it this way, Jesus is making himself equal with God.

Here you have a whole slew of confusion, like tangled hair uncombed for years. You have the man who believes, apparently with many others at the time, that a quick dip in some special water, "when the water is (mysteriously) stirred up," will heal him. You have some of the Jews who object to the healing because it was done on a Sabbath (but not, it seems, to all the paralytics dipping into the water to try to be healed at the same time). Finally, you have the man again who does not even seem to know who healed him, before Jesus reappears and tells him.

In contrast you have Jesus, who with a brief sentence ends the man's physical problems. It is almost as if the invalid is like us: waiting by a pool that we think will heal us (or help us), unable to get in because no one will help us (or carry us), and along comes Jesus, and—wham! All is made right at a word.

That does not mean there will never be any problems again for this invalid, or for invalids like us, because he needs to be told a little later in the story to "sin no more." Salvation and healing do not mean we are incapable of sinning or free from tribulations in life.

We are people who are naturally unable to see things as they are, to be as we should be; we are not seeing everything right; we do not naturally have the truth. The truth may be out there, but we cannot see it or find it or get it. It is not only that the scientific truth of the universe, the philosophical truth, the theological truth is so large that we cannot possibly contain it, or understand it, or know it. It is that our sense naturally of what is true is miscued; it is like a bad reception on an old radio that occasionally picks up true words from the sending station, but in between there is static, and sometimes even the words we hear are garbled by the faulty antenna in our minds and hearts. The WiFi is spotty.

We, like Matthew with his tax collector booth, tend to think that money is the answer or that there is no answer beyond "making a living"; we tend to live stuck by the pool of Bethesda, unmoving and not expecting help. We tend to think we deserve no better and expect no worse. Whereas the Big Picture about God, the Big Picture about the Bible, and the Big Picture about the World reveal that God is a God of blinding holiness, and yet, at the same time, he is Jesus who is the Lamb who takes away the sin of the world. He is the one who calls Matthew the tax collector to follow him; he is the "I Am" who is the door for us to be "saved." This is the truth, the truth that will set us free. And if you dumb it down, or make it feel trite inside, then you probably don't realize that the God of Abraham and Isaac and Jacob, the God who thundered from Mount Sinai with his law written with the finger of God, is also the God of Mount Zion, the God who provides salvation for those who fail to keep the law, invalids all.

SELF-DECEPTION

Perhaps the greatest barrier to following Jesus truly is the problem of self-deception. It is one thing to do something wrong and to know it, but it is quite another to have a pattern of wrongdoing (or being) and not to be aware of it at all. The latter difficulty is far trickier and more difficult to solve— self-deception. You find that Paul talks about it in his letter to the Romans, where he discusses how God "gave them up" to this or that behavior or attitude, how they became sufficiently entranced by it that they started to do it with less and less awareness of its unhealthiness. There are some, Paul says elsewhere, whose consciences have been seared as with an iron; few of us reading this will have gone to that extreme, but I suspect all of us have difficulties with being self-deceived at one level or another. That's why David prays, "Declare me innocent from hidden faults" (Psalm 19:12), because without God searching us and knowing us, we have very little hope of knowing ourselves truly at all.

The third letter of Jesus to the churches of Asia, the letter to Pergamum, reveals some of these difficulties of being self-deceived. Pergamum was a good church, and in fact, had resisted persecution so faithfully that one of its number (Antipas) had been faithful to death. He is called by Jesus "faithful witness," the word *witness* being the same word from which comes *martyr*—showing how quickly the idea of a martyr developed from that of witnessing to Jesus' message, even at risk of persecution, even at risk of death. This "faithfulness unto death" was what Jesus had urged upon Smyrna in the previous letter, and so for Pergamum to have achieved it, and not compromised, was certainly no small thing.

And yet there were difficulties—despite their great faithfulness, they had conceded ground in other, subtler areas. Here is the story as Jesus revealed it to John:

> And to the angel of the church in Pergamum write: "The words of him who has the sharp two-edged sword. I know where you dwell, where Satan's throne is. Yet you hold fast my name, and you did not deny my faith even in the days of Antipas my faithful witness, who was killed among you, where Satan dwells. But I have a few things against you: you have some there who hold the teaching of Balaam, who taught Balak to put a stumbling block before the sons of Israel, so that they might eat food sacrificed to idols and practice sexual immorality. So also you have some who hold the teaching of the Nicolaitans. Therefore repent. If not, I will come to you soon and war against them with the sword of my mouth. He who has an ear, let him hear what the Spirit says to the churches. To the one who conquers I will give some of the hidden manna, and I will give him a white stone, with a new name written on the stone that no one knows except the one who receives it." (Revelation 2:12-17)

Pergamum was called "Satan's throne" for several reasons, we think. First and foremost, Pergamum was the religious capital of Roman emperor worship in Asia. It was, therefore, grandiloquently the "throne of Satan," the place where worship of a mere human being was demonically transposed to the true worship of God. There were other allusions, though. For a traveler coming on the ancient road from Smyrna to Pergamum—the route that our letter would have traveled, we may presume—the citadel city of Pergamum looked unnervingly like a throne perched on a hill. What's more, the particular god of Pergamum had as its symbol the serpent, which, of course, for Christians steeped in the Scriptures, would have suggested Satan.

> Overcoming means receiving the truth. Following Jesus is the truth that sets us free.

Pergamum was a religious center not only for Roman emperor worship but also for this Pergamum god, for Zeus, and for others.

Here the faithful Pergamum Christians, especially Antipas of great renown, had stood their ground against some form of persecution. But now they faced a more difficult, in some ways, problem, one that they failed to diagnose or deal with. This was a "Balaam-like" problem—that is, referring to the famous false teacher of the Old Testament, who had been hired to curse the Israelites but, because of God's constraint, had instead blessed them. Still, he advised Moab's king to use a subtler approach: to seduce Israel with spiritual and sexual adultery. We do not know exactly what "the teaching of the Nicolaitans" was, though various ideas have been suggested. But we know that whatever it was, it was like this Balaam error: it was encouraging immorality by its teaching.

This was not an intellectually subtle error, a great doctrinal dispute that would take the greatest minds of the age to solve. Its subtlety lay in its appeal, the idea that faithfulness could be coupled with immorality, and in that sort of self-deception this Nicolaitan idea was making progress among the otherwise faithful community of Christians at Pergamum.

And the solution? The solution was the right truth, the word of God—as Jesus says. If there is not change (repentance, *metanoia*) soon, then he will come providentially with the true teaching of God's word, the "sword of [his] mouth." To those who listen to this truth, Jesus promises great things: "hidden manna" and a "white stone, with a new name written on the stone."

The "white stone" is an allusion with multiple references. This is a common literary technique of John's. He often writes in such a way as to evoke a whole rainbow of different vivid colors in the mind's eye. These multiple analogous references, though, do not mean there are many different possible meanings to his imagery. He has a single meaning, but he seeks to underline and evoke that meaning more powerfully by drawing upon different images, which speak more powerfully to some than others. Here, then, the "white stone" would have evoked several different images for the Pergamum believers. These small, pebblelike stones were used as ways of casting a vote. They were also used as tickets to banquets. Here they are white to indicate purity. They have a name, known only to those who receive it, to indicate intimacy. This is a personal invitation from Jesus to you and me.

Overcoming, then, for Pergamum Christians, as for all Christians, means receiving the truth: a constant supply of spiritual sustenance from Jesus to meet our daily needs ("hidden manna") and an intimacy of communion with Jesus (a "white stone")—both of which entail present blessing and also future entrance to glory. We have Jesus' vote and a ticket of entrance to the banquet of heaven.

Following Jesus, entering through the door, getting up and walking after him, receiving the "white stone" to find the truth—in him—is the truth that sets us free.

A Day for Freedom

"And whoever does not take his cross and follow me
is not worthy of me."

—*Matthew 10:38*

Weightlessness (or zero gravity) is the feeling of no longer being tied to the earth, but being able to float—as if in water, but more so—above the ground. It is a feeling that astronauts on the orbiting space station often experience, and it is a feeling that many of us have had in our dreams. All the heaviness of gravity "floats" away, and we are circling above the ground, free-falling.

Free-falling is actually, the scientists will tell us, a more accurate description for this experience of weightlessness because even on the space station there is not zero gravity (if there were, the orbiting satellite could float out into space). According to Newton's physics, the experience of zero gravity results from the satellite constantly falling toward the earth but going over the horizon, giving an extended feeling like free fall but more so. The so-called vomit comet, any plane that mimics the feeling of weightlessness for its occupants by an elliptical pathway, gives a similar opportunity for the feeling of weightlessness for its passengers, whether they be tourists, scientists, or moviemakers.

Weightlessness sounds wonderful, "freeing," releasing from the g-force of constantly being stuck with heaviness all around us and through us. Who doesn't like the feeling of floating comfortably in beautifully warm water, in a safe environment, warm sun dappling the water around? Who would not like the feeling of floating on an updraft like a bird, swooping and soaring to our hearts' content? Who would not like, at least for once, to experience weightlessness?

The trouble is that the body finds such freedom from weight to be a problem difficult to handle. In any extended experience of weightlessness, the body begins to lose muscle mass, even bone density. One astronaut, on return to earth, was asked to explain the feeling of heaviness that she now had in her life. She was given a pencil to pick up and asked how much she thought it weighed: she answered two pounds. It is said that a lengthy space trip with zero gravity, like a trip to Mars, could mean astronauts losing as much as 10 percent of bone mass. It is not just the potential inconvenience of watching your pencil floating away; it is coming to terms with actually needing to lift a two-pound pencil on your return to ground.

We were not made to float; we were made to walk, to run, to experience gravity constantly. After three weeks in a simulated zero-gravity situation, those conducting the experiment asked the human subjects what it was like to try to stand up in regular surroundings and were told it was like having a vise grip on their bodies.

The common idea of "freedom" is a freedom from all constraints, a moral zero gravity if you will, as long as such freedom does not hurt someone else. We dream about being free to be whomever we want, get whatever we want, be with whomever we want—whenever we want, however we want—as long as it does not hurt anyone else. When we were young, perhaps we dreamed about being the best football player ever, or the richest man in the world, or the most beautiful person. In this way such fantasies about freedom are a lot closer to dreams of power and conquest than we might always admit. Freedom is not just about being unconstrained; it is about the ability to be what we want to be. Perhaps that's why technology can be such a fascination for some of us. Apart from the nice, shiny feel of a new tool, it seems to promise us the ability to do more, have more, be more, than otherwise we could be without this latest gadget or gizmo.

Christians are all for freedom, when freedom is defined as being what we are meant to be. But if freedom is defined as moral weightlessness, a lack of any ethical barriers, or the dispensing with all good authority, then Christians are not for that kind of freedom. That kind of freedom is, Christians would say, not really freedom, any more than it is more freeing for a person to take a space walk without a space suit. It may be a constraint to "have to" wear a space suit, and in that sense, it may be more "freeing" not

"And whoever does not take his cross and follow me is not worthy of me."

to have to wear a space suit, but that kind of freedom means going into outer space unable to breathe, and that is not freedom worth the name. It is a freedom that leads to a far bigger, more serious constraint: death.

Paul, the apostle of freedom, tells the Galatians to stand firm and not let themselves be burdened again by a yoke of slavery, to not feel they have to perform certain religious rituals in order to be saved, but to realize that it is all by grace through faith alone. Yet this freedom is not total moral zero gravity, because he says, "Only do not use your freedom as an opportunity for the flesh" (Galatians 5:13). You are free, but don't think that means that it is a good idea to take your space suit off in outer space. You are free, but don't think it's a good idea to act in certain immoral ways, for the reality is that these still lead to not being able to breathe, to death. You are free, but it's the kind of freedom to be what you were meant to be. A goldfish in a goldfish bowl may be set free if it is taken out of the very small tank and put in a much bigger one. It may be set free if it is taken out of a very small tank and placed in a large pond, with all the right nutrients for its survival, the right climate, and without immediate danger of being consumed by some predator. All these ways may set a goldfish "free." But if you take your fish out of its too-small fish tank and simply dump it on the counter outside the goldfish bowl, in the "free" open air, you are no more setting it free than a man is free if he is sent on a space walk without a space suit, or a Christian is free if he or she has been set free, but then uses this freedom as an opening for the flesh. That is not freedom; it is trying to breathe out of water if you are a fish; it's death.

This may not be a popular truth in our age, when so many want to tell us, "You can be anything you want to be," but deep down we know that what we are talking about here is true. It is this sort of truth that is the truth that sets you free. That's why in the fourth of the seven "Follow me" sayings of Jesus from Matthew's Gospel, Jesus is such a realist, almost a hard-nosed realist. He says, "And whoever does not take his cross and follow me is not worthy of me."

Here Jesus is referring to taking up your cross on the road to execution, but it is more than the well-known idea that Jesus wants us to "die to self" by making Jesus Lord of our lives. The text is worth quoting in full, in its context:

> "Do not think that I have come to bring peace to the earth. I have not come to bring peace, but a sword. For I have come to set a man against his father, and a daughter against her mother, and a daughter-in-law against her mother-in-law. And a person's enemies will be those of his own household. Whoever loves father or mother more than me is not worthy of me, and whoever loves son or daughter more than me is not worthy of me. *And whoever does not take his cross and follow me is not worthy of me.* Whoever finds his life will lose it, and whoever loses his life for my sake will find it." (Matthew 10:34-39, my emphasis)

Not once does Jesus mention freedom (or fulfillment, prosperity, excitement, and a generally good time in the Christian tour of the Holy Land!). Instead his teaching here about what it means to follow him is marked by one shocking contrast, underlined by three "whoevers." The one shocking contrast is between "peace" and a "sword." Of those two, all of us would have thought that Jesus was on the side of peace, but it appears not to be so. He did not come to bring "peace on earth." This seems rather surprising given the well-known Christmas announcement of the angels that Jesus *had* come to bring peace on earth, but even this peace is only to "those with whom he is pleased" (Luke 2:14).

What Jesus is saying here in Matthew is not that he is for unmitigated physical aggression ("sword"), for Jesus clearly was not and taught his followers to turn the other cheek, but that following Jesus means realizing that not everyone will follow Jesus. There will be peace in some sense in this world for those who follow Jesus, but that peace will not be total, for there will be others—perhaps some very close to you—who will not follow Jesus. So the contrast between peace and sword is worked out between family members who follow Jesus and family members who do not follow Jesus.

Which brings us to the three "whoevers" of the passage: the first is about family, the second about shame, and the third about life and death. Jesus is saying that family (father/mother, son/daughter) is less important than following him; we cannot "love" them more. Jesus is saying that the ultimate shame of being seen to carry a cross, and therefore be on the road to the brutal Roman criminal execution, is something less important, and worth having, for the sake of following Jesus. He is saying that following him is about losing your life in order to find it rather than trying to find it (in which case you will lose it).

This is not just that following Jesus means putting Jesus first; it is saying that following Jesus means putting Jesus *only*. In ancient times the family was a much more authoritative force in many people's lives than it is today. The family controlled your destiny; the head of a Roman family—the *paterfamilias*—was a powerful, if sometimes benign, dictator. To run from that to follow Jesus was an extraordinary demand, a bar set very high indeed. The cross was death and ignominy. The life, or soul, the very being of who you are, was put to one side in order to find that the life, or soul, was Jesus himself. This is quite a series of claims.

In other words, Jesus is the air you breathe, the water you swim in: he is freedom, life, family. He is God, but not the pagan god of Roman culture, nor the rather tame, conventional, cultural God who baptizes all our Western values as his own and does not threaten the status quo or ask very much of us. This is the God of the Bible, the God who says "Follow me," and not anything or anyone else (even your own life).

How can this be? To understand this, it is helpful to grasp the Bible's attitude toward slavery and freedom, which is rather different from our approach to these two realities—one much desired, the other hated—of human existence.

SLAVERY TO SINNERS

What Jesus says or does comes against the background of the Exodus, the most important event in human history for God's people Israel, and the story that Jesus is referring to, or reenacting, or fulfilling in his own person and life. Jesus is far more than just another Moses, of course; we have seen that in his "I Am" statements. But the narrative of the Exodus is the grand narrative, the metanarrative, the big story, against which much of what Jesus does is understood—from the Passover to his death as the Passover Lamb to the way in which he viewed God's people as needing the sort of rescuing that God provided through Moses to the Old Testament people of God.

This was described in the Old Testament more in terms of the rescue of people from sinners, rather than as a rescue of people from sin, and part of what happens in the New Testament is that the model of the Exodus becomes not so much a model of physical rescue from captivity (from sinners) as a rescue from sin—which indeed can include sinners as much as sin. You see this interpretation going on in the famous speech of the first Christian martyr, Stephen, where he surveys the whole history of God's people and concludes, with a total lack of diplomacy, that the people in front of him were being just as resistant to God's work as all the people who had gone before them. What he is saying is that in opposing Jesus and the followers of Jesus, you are actually doing exactly what your forefathers did in opposing other prophets beforehand; God's people are being rescued, they are Egypt, and God's people are coming out to worship. "I have surely seen the affliction of my people who are in Egypt, and have heard their groaning, and I have come down to deliver them" (Acts 7:34). "Let my people go," God says to Pharaoh, and he will, ultimately through the work of Jesus, more than another Moses.

Stephen is killed not so much for telling the Old Testament story of God's people in a way that led up to the Messiah being Jesus, though surely that was not popular, for these were people who had helped execute Jesus. Stephen was killed for deliberately saying that the people in front of him were like all the Old Testament people of God who had rebelled against God's law—they had "received the law as delivered by angels and did not keep it" (Acts 7:53). The message of many of the Old Testament prophets was that God's people had been rescued from Egypt, but they had taken much of Egypt with them, including a desire for Egypt's way of worship. They had constantly longed to go back to Egypt, even though they had been slaves there. You can take God's people out of Egypt, but you can't take Egypt out of God's people, at least not without the much more radical surgery that God will himself bring through Jesus.

It is not so much that the exile and return from Babylon had not fully happened yet, and that they felt the need for a real return from exile. It is not so much that, Stephen says, but that the whole history of God's people—shaped by the covenants to Abraham, Isaac, and Jacob, formed together by the rescue through Moses out of Egypt—that whole history they did not make "work." They received the law but did not keep it. We are not to imagine Stephen with an angry face and pointy finger when he says, "You did not keep the law!"; "How awful you are!" No, Stephen is describing the reality, that a rescue from sinners (this external slavery) is incomplete unless it also includes a rescue from sin (not only receiving the law but finding the power, the freedom, to obey it).

The same connection between the Exodus and Jesus' mission to free us from sin and sinners is made in the fourth of

> The life that Jesus offers, by us taking up our crosses and submitting to his way, is true life and true freedom

Jesus' seven signs in John's Gospel. It occurs in chapter 6, this famous story of Jesus feeding five thousand with five loaves and two fish. The people are asked to sit, Jesus gives thanks, and the food is distributed to them all, with twelve basketfuls left over. Then, "when the people saw the sign that he had done, they said, 'This is indeed the Prophet who is to come into the world!'" (John 6:14).

They misunderstand what that means, however, and Jesus sees they are about to make him king by force, and so he withdraws from them to the mountain by himself. Later, on the other side of the sea, after Jesus has walked on water to rejoin his disciples, the crowd finds him again. Jesus discerns that they are interested in him because of his miracle of making enough bread for five thousand people, and then he says the first of the seven "I Am" sayings that we looked at on Monday ("I am the bread of life").

In between he says this: "Truly, truly, I say to you, it was not Moses who gave you the bread from heaven, but my Father gives you the true bread from heaven. For the bread of God is he who comes down from heaven and gives life to the world" (John 6:32-33).

He goes on to explain that whoever eats of this "bread of life" is a true follower (that is, whoever believes in Jesus, trusts him, and has a connection personally with him). Throughout the New Testament, and its interpretation and fulfillment of the Old Testament, there is this idea, this vision, of us as people rescued out of Egypt and journeying to the Promised Land, feeding on the manna, the bread of heaven, in relationship with Jesus himself.

Slavery to Sin

So the freedom that we have from Jesus, offered to us through faith in him, when we are "eating the bread of life," is not just simply a physical freedom from oppression to sinners, a physical freedom from slavery in Egypt. It can include this, and in the Old Testament it did mean this, but it is more than this. Of course, in the final rescue of God's people, when we enter the "Promised Land," there will be a freedom that is physical as well as spiritual, a new heaven and a new earth, the home of righteousness, a whole new universe, but it will be populated by people who have not only been taken out of Egypt but who have also had Egypt taken out of them.

The life, then, that Jesus wants us not to find but lose, in order that we find (true) life in his name, is a life that stretches back to and counters the myths and lies of Egypt, and further still all the way to the myths and lies of the garden of Eden. Ever since then, our "life" was corrupted to be a self-focused life, a life that viewed freedom as a fish out of water, a man on a space walk without a space suit, "death," not freedom as being all that we were designed to be (in Jesus' name, and in God's will, both in creation and New Creation). This life, the life that he warns us not to try to find, is actually not life, but death. Instead, the life that he offers, by us taking up our crosses and submitting to his way, is true life and true freedom, for it is a death to the life that is not true living, a life that is really trying to breathe in outer space without a space suit.

Consider why it is that people do not follow Jesus. This seems to be a problem that few of our teachers and thinkers have given as much attention as it deserves, for if Jesus is clearly the way, the truth, and the life, if he is the Savior of the world, and if the Bible is true and his way is true freedom, then why is it that not everyone follows him? Of course, the ultimate answer is that only those who are called by God follow him, as Paul outlines in Romans 9. Not everyone is destined for life, which is true, and a most profound truth, but it does not answer what it is at the basic level of emotion and thinking that goes through someone's mind when he or she rejects Jesus.

Another, also true, answer is that some people do not follow Jesus because they have not had the opportunity to do so (though in our day of mass communication, that number is smaller every moment). Again, at the most basic and profound level, we come back to the will of God, who decides how things should be. If we inquire on what basis he chooses some and not others, and whether there is a reason for it in our disposition or our behavior, then we are really saying that the reason is not in God's choice but in a certain characteristic of our own. The Old Testament people of Israel were not chosen because they were greater, more numerous, or better than the others. We as Christians are not chosen for our own merits, but out of God's pure grace and favor. We all rightly deserve judgment, and that God reaches out to us is pure mercy, undeserved. If that is unfair, then fairness is all of us being rejected; it is mercy, which means that it resides purely in the mercy of God, his compassionate will, not in our merits or abilities.

But what happens in our hearts and minds when we reject the call to follow Jesus? All who believe in him, the Bible tells us, will be saved. Whoever hears the call and follows Jesus is a disciple.

So why is it that some do not? What, in this sense of "why," is going on in their hearts and minds? Often it is an issue of freedom. We dream not only of floating up high, with zero physical gravity, but also with zero moral gravity. Shame is a powerful force in society that prevents us from doing many things that otherwise at least a part of us would want to do. If shame or social disapproval were removed, then what would we wish to do in our freedom? And who is there to prevent that? Above all stands one fierce voice, shaking our souls to their very depths, the Judge, the Lord, the Holy of Holies, and without him, we can surely do as we like.

The more sensitive—and honest—thinkers have admitted that this desire for moral freedom, if not moral zero gravity as long as no one else is hurt, played a large part in their rejection of Jesus and of God. In his *Being and Nothingness*, for instance, Jean-Paul Sartre made an argument that has been summarized as, "If God exists, then I am not free. But I *am* free; therefore God does not exist." You need to hear the growl over the word "am" in the phrase "but I *am* free." It is an assertion of independence, and in that sense freedom. The Bloomsbury Group was a loosely affiliated set of thinkers and writers and artists connected by a desire to forge a new way forward intellectually, socially, even morally. The Bloomsbury Group admitted that much of their revolt against God and traditional ways of thinking and traditional morality was because they wanted the freedom to experiment, to be morally free in that sense. God was in the way of this so-called progress, and so God was removed from their way of thinking in life.

The same is true at a much larger level and grander scale: God is the protector of many of us from the uninhibited "freedom" of the maliciously powerful, for whom God is an inconvenient meddler in their desire for domination, wealth, and exploitation of everyone else. Evil elite forces desire more and more and more, and the only force capable in the world of judging these nefarious demi-gods of the modern age, rich beyond imagining and with enormous power, is the One True God. Only he can reign in their "freedom," their zero moral gravity. And so he is dispensed with, argued against, denied. Who else is the protector of the widow, the orphan, the righteous? This is the point that is made in Dostoyevsky's *Brothers Karamazov*, where he writes that once a religious foundation for society is dismissed, "everything is permitted."[1] It is perhaps not by accident that one of the most famous memoirs of the Holocaust, Elie Wiesel's *Night*, picks up on this same phrase when father and son grapple with the reality of having just seen babies burnt alive in the ovens at Auschwitz: "Today, everything is possible."[2] Without God, we are free to do whatever we want—but that freedom is the freedom of Auschwitz, as close to hell as the twentieth century experienced.

Free From

Of course, this is not normally how submission to God is viewed, even by some believers, as that which guarantees our freedom. Rather, submission to God is often seen as the very opposite of freedom. How can I be free and follow Jesus? Surely the very fact that I am *following* someone other than myself means that I am not free. Freedom is freedom from all external constraints, and the ability to be free from all internal doubts, and instead able to do exactly as I please. Submission to God—following Jesus, in that sense—is then, we normally would think, the very opposite of freedom because it means, well, not being free to do what we want, not being free from what someone else wants us to do.

But actually that is to assume that people are already free, and that to submit to God means to become unfree. All of our worries, our confusions, our distrust of the biblical idea of freedom as following Jesus comes down to a misunderstanding of human nature. Look at it like this: if I am in prison and someone comes to set me free, he opens the door and then says, "Follow me," am I likely to say, "No, I am not going to follow you because that would make me unfree, for then I would be following someone else other than myself"? No, I would get up and follow him. That is why Jesus says he has come for the sinners, not the righteous; that is, he has come for those who realize that they are in moral prison, rather than those who dream that they are outside, running in the wide-open fields of moral freedom already.

What if, on the other hand, I am living the life of Riley,

a phrase meaning the prosperous, happy life? What if I am living in a well-made, expansive mansion, with servants and opportunities for achievement? What if I have a grand piano in the drawing room, expensive Renoir masterpieces in the living room, and a gold sparkling chandelier hanging over the stairway? In short, I am doing fine, thank you very much. If this is my situation and someone knocks at the door, opens it, and says, "Leave all this and come follow me," I might say, "No thanks! I'm already free. Why would I want to submit myself to you and become unfree?"

It all comes down to how we see ourselves, how we view where we are naturally. Do we think, morally and spiritually speaking, we are in a mansion of glory already, not needing rescuing, and certainly not needing freeing? Or do we think that we are in a prison, morally and spiritually speaking, and therefore being asked to follow our rescuer as he leads the way out is not slavery—the very reverse!—but freedom?

How do we decide where we are? Which of these two caricatures is most like our own situation, morally speaking? The Bible makes it clear that it is the latter, being spiritually in prison.

"None is righteous, no, not one" (Romans 3:10).

"The wages of sin is death" (Romans 6:23).

Adam and Eve were expelled from the garden, and the sentence of death fell upon them and all their heirs ever since. In Psalm 51:5, David says, "I was brought forth in iniquity, and in sin did my mother conceive me." He is referring not just to his own life but also to all people, as representative in his personal confession of the situation of the human race. So for

Jesus now to say, "Follow me; take up your cross; die to self,"—
in other words, "Submit to my way"—he is not taking away our
freedom by that means; he is actually giving us our freedom:
"Come and serve the Master, he alone is true; he will pardon
sinners, therefore pardon you; He has promised power, power
to all who ask; power to conquer Satan, power for every task."[3]

The prison door swings open. "Come and serve the Master," as this old chorus puts it, and the path toward freedom is
open before us. "Stand firm therefore, and do not submit again
to a yoke of slavery," Paul says in Galatians 5:1. And in Romans
5:1-2, "Therefore, since we have been justified by faith, we have
peace with God through our Lord Jesus Christ. Through him
we have also obtained access by faith into this grace in which
we stand, and we rejoice in hope of the glory of God."

Human experience tells us that this is the human condition, that we need setting free by a Master, not that we are
free already and need to resist
being enslaved. This is not
merely the old adage to "sow
a thought, reap a deed; sow a
deed, reap a habit; sow a habit,
reap a destiny," though there is
much truth to the ingrained
power of habit and how hard it
is to train in a different direction once a habit has been set.

> The only power
> that can break
> us from the
> most consuming
> addictions is the
> call to follow Jesus
> and die to that self.

But it is more than that. In Christ, and by his Spirit, we now
have the freedom to break those habits, a work of our entire
lives though that often is.

But outside of Christ? The habits tend to grow and grow; our prison becomes darker and smaller, more prisonlike, as our minds and hearts close in upon themselves until finally we squeeze into the darkness.

Alfred Kinsey made it his life work to research human sexuality. He, many say, provided the intellectual credibility required for the sexual revolution of the 1960s and on. His books—one on male sexual behavior, the other on female—were known collectively as the Kinsey Reports. They relied heavily upon interviewing individuals and constructing estimates of certain kinds of sexual behavior based on those interviews. It has long been apparent that Kinsey's work was profoundly flawed and deeply personal, even though it is still defended.[4] Nonetheless, it was presented as credibly scientific, and it still influences what is and is not viewed as permissible today. Long before Kinsey, the aesthete Oscar Wilde quipped that the only way to defeat temptation was to give in to it. But Oscar Wilde died penniless in Paris, stuck in his habit of making the bitter sweet and the sweet bitter, finally ceding voicelessly to the administration of last rites from a Roman Catholic priest.[5]

Sexual addiction represents a classic example of the kind of problems we can fall into when we do not follow Jesus and his teaching, but instead think we are more "free" when we do whatever we want. This is a misunderstanding of human nature, at its most basic, that if we sow a thought, reap a deed, sow a habit, we then reap a destiny. Addictions, not only to sex but also to alcohol, career, fame, even to power itself, create a prison as sure as any physical cage. And the only power in the universe that can break us from those most consuming addictions is the call to follow Jesus, take up our cross, and die to that self.

These are not merely external idols that we worship, though these addictions that enslave us can certainly seem like obsessions. But they are not *merely* that; that is too simple a way of looking at the problem, and it can cast the blame on the idol, not us. We are attracted to the idol because there is already an idol in our hearts. We are psychologically, "soul-ish-ly," bound. And only Christ can set us free. This is something that Kinsey appears never to have understood, and it is something that our culture today, and therefore many of us who are influenced by it, also fails to grasp. The culture thinks we are free when we are free from moral constraints, the moral zero gravity of life without submission to God, and without following Jesus; but all that is digging deeper into the darkness: the thought, the deed, the habit, the destiny. And Jesus' call to follow him is a call out of the darkness and into the light, at the expense of the sacrifice of our self, the self that is bound to darkness. To submit to Jesus and follow him, all I give him is my sin, and everything I receive is grace and mercy.

It's a deal that no one could refuse, if an individual understands the true condition of his or her heart, the true nature of humanity.

FREE TO

That's why in Jesus' fourth "I Am" statement in John's Gospel, he compares himself to a shepherd, and all others to thieves. There is no utterly neutral moral or spiritual realm where we can be "free," in the sense of weightless; but rather there are competing forces within and without us, and he is the Good Shepherd. "The thief comes only to steal and kill and destroy. I came that they may have life and have it abundantly. *I am the good shepherd*" (John 10:10-11, emphasis added). He is come not to enslave us but to set us free (from) and free to (life, abundantly). "I am the good shepherd. The good shepherd lays down his life for the sheep." Unlike a hired hand, also meant to protect the sheep from thieves and wolves but not personally involved, this Good Shepherd is willing to put his life at risk and give his life for our protection.

These are familiar ideas, perhaps, but in the context of freedom and slavery, they take on a new life and meaning. When Jesus says, "Follow me," he is referring us to who he is, and that, in part, is this Good Shepherd. We are not following someone who will take advantage of us or spoil us or ruin us or leave us stranded when the going gets tough. We are following someone who is going to see it through all the way to Calvary—that is how much it will cost him to set us free. And it is that Shepherd we are to follow.

This is not simply moving out of prison, it is moving onwards and upwards, with Christ ahead, us following, hearing his voice, listening to his word, and becoming those who live life abundantly. As such, this is far *more* than many of our ideas of freedom from captivity or prison. We tend to think of being set free purely in terms of "freedom from" rather than "freedom to." We think of some of the great historic moments of freedom politically—the fall of the Berlin Wall or the breaking of apartheid in South Africa—and while the freedom that was gained was immense and stunning ("freedom from"), after the wall had fallen down, after apartheid had ended, in many ways the hard work of reconciliation and truth was only just beginning. It took negotiation, compromise, time, and effort. Many of the old ideas, the pain, the bitterness, the jealousies, and the anger from the injustices of the past carried on and remained with the now recently "freed" people, such that they wondered at times how "free" they had really become (in the sense of "free to").

One way of looking at this is by way of Bob Dylan's controversial song from his early years, "The Hurricane." In the song Dylan tells the legendary story of a man arrested by the police for a murder of which he was innocent. This man was a champion boxer at the time of his arrest, but by the end of the time in jail, his opportunity had gone. It is a prophetic song, a song of pace and passion and power, singing of how this man—Rubin Carter—was incarcerated but then finally set free. Whether all the details of the song are true or not, Carter was at last released in the 1980s and all charges of murder then dropped. Yet, though he was "free from" now—he was no longer in prison—he still could not retrieve those years that had been wasted. One time he could have been the champion of the world, but now he was an old man, and his time had gone.

It was made into a movie with Denzel Washington in 1999, and the basic theme of Dylan's song was followed, though many say there is another side to the story. Whatever the facts in this case, the version as told by Dylan illustrates a point: you can be set free from prison, but the time has gone; you can't relive the years that have passed. You can be free from, but it is another thing to be free to, to become a new person with new opportunities. Not even just to get "the time back," but to be changed in the motivations and actions of the heart, and therefore of the body, so that you become not only "free from" whatever has plagued you, but "free to" become the man or woman you were meant to be.

That's a whole different level of freedom, but it is the freedom that Jesus offers: to soar on high, to have the life abundant. To follow him—not just out of the prison but as the Good Shepherd, the "I Am" who has everything on offer that we need and more than we could dream of—is true freedom now and perfectly for all eternity. This real freedom is a powerful antidote, when properly understood and internalized, to the spiritual malaise of feeling we will miss out if we radically follow Jesus.

In fact, following Jesus is not only freedom *from*, it is freedom *to*. Freedom to listen to the Shepherd's voice, freedom to follow him, freedom to "lie down in green pastures," to "walk through the valley of the shadow of death" but still have him there to comfort and protect us. It is freedom to have "oil" overflow, to have joy. It is freedom that completes all the ideas from David's famous Shepherd Psalm, which Jesus deliberately compares himself to. The Lord is my Shepherd; who is the Shepherd? "I am," Jesus says.

> The LORD is my shepherd; I shall not want.
>   He makes me lie down in green pastures.
> He leads me beside still waters.
>   He restores my soul.
> He leads me in paths of righteousness

for his name's sake.
Even though I walk through the valley
of the shadow of death,
I will fear no evil,
for you are with me;
your rod and your staff,
they comfort me.
You prepare a table before me
in the presence of my enemies;
you anoint my head with oil;
my cup overflows.
Surely goodness and mercy shall follow me
all the days of my life,
and I shall dwell in the house of the LORD
forever. (Psalm 23)

This is the same God (Jesus) who has set us "free from" as well as "free to."

TRULY FREE

Real freedom, and the shepherding of Jesus that provides it, is a background to the fourth the seven letters to the churches of Asia in the Book of Revelation. To understand this, we need to know something of the story into which the letter from Jesus lands, like an e-mail with a bright red exclamation point (!) next to it, to indicate that it is important and urgent and needs to be read and followed up on right now.

Thyatira was not a particularly remarkable city. It was certainly not a New York or DC or London; it was a small city that had nearly always been ruled by foreign invaders. Situated in a valley between two other valleys, its geopolitical circumstances afforded it no protection against foreign invasion. As such, its history reads like one subjugation after another. Because of its geographical vulnerability, it was always a garrison town, a place dominated by the military stationed there for its defense. In effect, it became an outpost for the kingdom based forty miles down the road in the capital, Pergamum.

There were also an astonishing number of trade guilds present in Thyatira. These commercial associations worshiped a particular pagan god and collaborated to support one another in the trade to which the society was dedicated. For, while Thyatira was a city that had been conquered by other powers, once the Roman Empire became established, and the famous *Pax Romana* brought peace to the ancient world, its very vulnerability to traffic became a source of strength for trade. Soon after the time of the letter, Thyatira became a powerful trading center. At around the time the letter would have been received, it was developing that way, as is evidenced, for instance, by Lydia, who was converted through the ministry of Paul in Philippi as recorded in the Acts of the Apostles, and Lydia was a trader in purple cloth from Thyatira. She also had a house in Philippi, indicating the growing spread and strength of the trade organizations of Thyatira across the ancient world even to Macedonia.

Military conquest and growing trade prominence—such was Thyatira. And it provided unique and troubling challenges to the Christians. Because being a member of a trade guild was the only way to advance in the world, Christians would have been easily tempted to become members of these organizations. After all, why not? They knew the idols that were worshiped were nothing. And if they did not become members of a trade guild, their livelihoods would rapidly diminish to the point of poverty. However, if they did join a trade guild, they would need to engage in the pagan festivals that periodically took place, where meat that had been offered to idols was consumed at the tables as a present from the god, and where, after the meal had ended, more immoral activities were the expected norm.

Into this situation of perplexing conflict between the world and the church, Jezebel provided what seemed like a ready answer. Jezebel, a pseudonym either for a teaching or a person, implying her derivation from the Old Testament Jezebel, who led Israel astray to pagan gods, taught something like this: "We know that idols are nothing, and we know that grace is stronger than sin, so go to the festivals of the trade guilds; be involved, for even 'the deep things of Satan' will not tarnish your profession of faith. Indeed, you'll be strengthened in your devotion by knowing these things and still believing in Jesus."

It was, in other words, a teaching saying that moral compromise with the world need not compromise salvation. Or, as we might put it, that freedom from the world could include freedom to do whatever you want; that liberty was really about permissiveness, not about being who you were meant to be. Fish, jump out of the water and breathe on dry land! Astronaut, take off your

> Following Jesus means taking up our cross and dying to self. *That is freedom.*

space suit and breathe in outer space! Christian, don't follow Christ's moral teachings; do what you want! That's freedom!

Except it is not. It is a return to slavery.

And so Jesus comes along with this letter to Thyatira:

> And to the angel of the church in Thyatira write: "The words of the Son of God, who has eyes like a flame of fire, and whose feet are like burnished bronze. I know your works, your love and faith and service and patient endurance, and that your latter works exceed the first. But I have this against you, that you tolerate that woman Jezebel, who calls herself a prophetess and is teaching and seducing my servants to practice sexual immorality and to eat food sacrificed to idols. I gave her time to repent, but she refuses to repent of her sexual immorality. Behold, I will throw her onto a sickbed, and those who commit adultery with her I will throw into great tribulation, unless they repent of her works, and I will strike her children dead. And all the churches will know that I am he who searches mind and heart, and I will give to each of you according to your works. But to the rest of you in Thyatira, who do not hold this teaching, who have not learned what some call the deep things of Satan, to you I say, I do not lay on you any other burden. Only hold fast what you have until I come. The one who conquers and who keeps my works until the end, to him I will give authority over the nations, and he will rule them with a rod of iron, as when earthen pots are broken in pieces, even as I myself have received authority from my Father. And I will give him the morning star. He who has an ear, let him hear what the Spirit says to the churches.'" (Revelation 2:18-29)

Jesus, as at the start of these letters, is the one with "eyes like a flame of fire"; he is the one who sees, who knows. The deeds and actions of the Christians at Thyatira cannot be hidden from him. He knows everything; he sees and he calls for repentance. If they do not repent, there will be consequences. The bed of adultery will become the bed of suffering; some sickness will strike down those who have given in to the false idea of liberty and freedom and turned their backs on following Jesus in this area of their lives. These "deep things of Satan," these esoteric secrets of the mystery cults, which were infecting the Roman Empire at the time with guarantees of some occult insight that could be achieved or discovered—for those who have not fallen into that trap, Jesus promises wonderful things. He lays no other burden upon them. They only have to hold on to him and their relationship with him. And for them there will be authority, a sharing in the kingdom of God through Jesus, his "rule" (or literally shepherding) of all the nations. They will be given the morning star, that is, Jesus himself, as the Book of Revelation later makes clear (22:16).

So the promises of moral weightlessness seem now not only pathetic but positively dangerous. They are Jezebel-like voices. The Kinsey Reports. The moral zero gravity of liberation, which is no liberty at all. Following Jesus does mean taking up our cross (yes), and dying to self (yes), *and that is freedom*. Not because of some pseudopious nonsense, but as the real freedom, whose beauty is seen by comparison with the lies of the freedom that is no freedom. The more we focus on ourselves, the deeper we dig into the darkness of the prison cell of doing "just what we want," the more pathetic, in every sense of the word, we become. We diminish; we rest our lives upon no other foundation but our own—small, petty, puny, and imprisoned: the destiny for which we sow thoughts, deeds, and habits; the human nature genetically skewed since before time immemorial (traces of our Adam heritage in ourselves, in our psyche, in our body, in chauvinistic jingoism, and in personality-driven ambitions); the deep things, the so-called free things, the things of Satan.

With a gasp of joy come the things of Christ—real freedom, for "if the Son sets you free, you will be free indeed" (John 8:36). A freedom from, a freedom to, a freedom to be who you are meant to be, no longer imprisoned, but following Jesus.

A Day for Humility

Then Jesus told his disciples, "If anyone would come after me,
let him deny himself and take up his cross and follow me."

—*Matthew 16:24*

It strikes me as ironic that two of the most memorable stories about humility come from men who are seldom thought to be. Winston Churchill (rarely if ever accused of being self-effacing) once said of Clement Attlee, his political rival and predecessor in the office of prime minister of Great Britain: "He was a modest man who has much to be modest about."

This famous putdown, along with many of Churchill's others, has entered folklore, and influences how at least some of us think about humility. Humility, we think, is "modesty"; it is bending over backward not to push yourself forward; it is being less than you could be for the sake of others so they can be all that they would wish to be.

There are literary caricatures that make this picture of Christian humility even less appealing. Perhaps most compellingly in Charles Dickens's *David Copperfield*, the villain, Uriah Heep, constantly tells anyone who will listen that he is ever so "'umble." But he is nothing of the sort; he is really filled with personal ambition and greed and tries to scheme his way to take over his master's business.

Ever so "'umble" or "modest," such ideas inform the way we look at statements like the one at the opening of this chapter, the fifth of Jesus' statements in Matthew's Gospel about what it means to follow him. Is Jesus telling us to not be ourselves? To be less than ourselves? After all, he does say that we are to deny ourselves, and surely this is the same thing. A Freudian analyst might have a field day with a patient who came in saying that he had spent his life denying himself. It sounds like Uriah Heep, or at least an unhealthy psychology. We need to learn to express ourselves, not repress ourselves.

What is Jesus talking about? The difficulty of finding out what it means to deny yourself, to be truly humble in a Christian-following-Jesus-denying-yourself sense, is emphasized by a story about Charles Spurgeon, the other man with a memorable quotation about humility and, as the greatest preacher of his day, also rarely accused of modesty. He is said to have written an article on humility under the title, "Humility and How I Attained It." Spurgeon, unlike Uriah Heep, was being thoroughly tongue in cheek in an irrepressibly Spurgeon-like way, but it does emphasize the difficulty again.

Is humility something that by its very nature is not attainable? If I think I am humble, then surely I am not, and so therefore I must never be able to be humble or think that I am. This seems like asking someone to run a race but telling him that he can never finish it, at least in this life. You can deny yourself, but if you ever think you have succeeded in denying yourself, or even worse, begin to feel pleased in yourself that you have denied yourself, then you can be sure that you are even further away than when you began.

This sort of tortuous, unending difficulty with the Christian life can be off-putting to many people and cause some atheists to wave banners saying, "God probably doesn't exist. Relax. Enjoy yourself." Enjoy your*self*! No, deny yourself. But does enjoying yourself and denying yourself really contradict each other? Can you deny yourself *and* enjoy yourself? Could it even be that denying yourself is the way to enjoying yourself fully and truly?

C. S. Lewis came closer to the real spirit of Christian humility when he wrote that humility has been made unattractive to many people because it seems to mean a clever man saying he is stupid or a beautiful woman thinking she is ugly. These being patently impossible things to do, humility becomes an unappealing virtue, if virtue by these standards it be. Instead, for Lewis, humility is not putting yourself down; it is simply not thinking about yourself at all. He writes that if you ever met a truly humble person, you would not think, *Wow! There goes a humble man*; instead, you would be more likely to think, *There is someone who seems to take a genuine interest and delight in other people*. That, for Lewis, is humility: others-focused (and presumably, ultimately, God-focused).[1]

Disagreeing with C. S. Lewis, especially when he is talking about humility, might seem the ultimate in pride, and yet as helpful as C. S. Lewis's definition of humility obviously is, there are still some weaknesses. Particularly in this call of Jesus to follow him, he does not say, "Ignore yourself"; he says, "Deny yourself," or "refuse" or "reject" yourself. Whether this verse is the perfect biblical description of humility or not, it certainly has something significant to say about it, and here Jesus is not telling us to forget ourselves. He is telling us we've got to deal with ourselves, deny ourselves in particular.

PLAGUE OF ARROGANCE

No one, I suppose, wants to be thought of as arrogant, but if arrogance is pride gone to seed, then we have a lot of it around today. Pride puffs up with views of ourselves. It is building our lives upon ourselves, and high thoughts of ourselves. Arrogance takes this to another level by turning the DNA of pride into a virus that is replicable and can be quickly caught by others. While pride can be quiet, even hidden, arrogance is boastful and proud of its pride. Arrogance is pride marketed to produce more pride; it is a bit like the plague once it gets going.

When I say "plague of arrogance," I am referring to the way today that we are taught to think of ourselves positively. Children are constantly told that they are great at almost everything they do; they are rarely exposed to the reality check of healthy criticism. There are no losers in competitions. People do not fail anymore; they merely achieve deferred success. We are born into the world with a naturally pretty strong view of ourselves already. Babies cry for milk, and they bawl for attention; we tend to feel from day one that we are rightly at the center of the universe. This tendency toward positive thinking means that many of us (especially in America) have grown up being told that we are "the best," that we can "be all that we want to be," that we can "do whatever we want," that any dream is attainable. At the same time educational standards in the Western world are slipping, and few of us

> The Bible actually assumes that we do love ourselves. What it does not assume is that we have learned to deny ourselves.

are actually the best at any of the hard skills of mathematics or writing or science anymore. With this prevalence of positive thinking, Roy Baumeister's research shows no correlation between high self-esteem and elevated educational or professional performance.[2] Instead, Jean Twenge documents a rise in narcissism.[3]

The Christian version of this is the idea that in order to love other people, we must first of all learn to "love ourselves." Did not Jesus say that we need to love our neighbor as we love ourselves? This must mean that we cannot love our neighbor *until* we love ourselves. And so in one quick move, Jesus' point that we need to work hard at loving our neighbors becomes Christianized psychobabble for working hard at loving ourselves.

The Bible actually assumes that we do love ourselves. What it does not assume is that we have learned to deny ourselves. Christians have a theology of human identity that means that we greatly value ourselves, and everyone else, because we are all made in the image of God. We also are realists about ourselves and our possibilities and potential in this life because we know that all humans since the Fall are tainted and marred and naturally warped. So we value humans in the image of God, and yet we are also realists about humans as fallen creatures now. This means that we do not think we can achieve every dream, or "climb every mountain," or be whoever we want to be. Instead, we think that we are of immense value, and also that this value will never be fully expressed or experienced in this life because we are fallen. About ourselves we are realist-idealists. We don't have "positive thinking"; we have truth, and we have love.

What's more, this image is in the image of God, which brings us back to what Jesus is saying in his command to follow him and deny ourselves and take up our crosses. It is the antidote to the plague of arrogance. He is recognizing the greatness of humanity by calling *us* to follow him. He is not overlooking us. He does not see us kicking in our blood and pass by on the other side (see Ezekiel 16:6). He comes for us. We are his creation; he loves us. His valuing of us is immense, incalculable, beyond price: it is valued as the price of God becoming human, God being incarnate, God humbling himself in Christ and becoming obedient, even unto death, even death on a cross. That is how much he values us as being made in his image, the image of God, when he calls out and says, "Follow me."

But he is also a realist: this calling to follow him, take up our crosses, and deny ourselves cuts at the root of arrogance. It is a saying like an antiviral drug, intending to come in and deal with the virus of arrogance and kill the DNA of pride at its core.

Perhaps few of us are truly arrogant. We are kind and think of others and do the right thing and bake cookies for our neighbors, but who among us is truly humble? Who is truly denying themselves and taking up their crosses? Pride is a bit like having HIV. HIV may not lead to full-blown AIDS, any more than pride might lead to arrogance, but they are connected, and with the HIV of pride, a remedy and intervention is essential.

NOT PUTTING YOURSELF DOWN

I cannot say I am an expert in humility, but I guess like most people, I know a thing or two about pride. What makes pride so HIV-like, in a spiritual sense, is that it stops us, certainly in the full-blown-AIDS-arrogance form, from getting the help we need. Pride is a disease that cuts us off from other people, that makes our natural/spiritual defense weaker, so that people with pride tend to be people with other spiritual ailments as well. If you have pride, you are more likely to feel jealous toward someone else's achievements because you feel that you deserve them. If you have pride, you are more likely to feel angry toward someone else because you cannot imagine yourself behaving as badly as that person did. If you have pride, you are more likely to feel bitter toward someone because you find it hard to believe that you could have done the same thing that he or she did to hurt you.

Pride stops us from seeking help because we are too proud to ask for it. Our pride tells us we should be able to handle these things alone. Given the predominance of pride as a human problem, could we say that pride is the cause of all evil? Making any one sin the source of all other sins is unwarranted unless the Bible specifically says so, and in fact, the Bible suggests that other problems lie at the root of our human condition. For instance, "the love of money is a root of all kinds of evils" (1 Timothy 6:10). Now, this well-known passage does not mean that money is the root of all evil, but that the *love* of money is the root of *all kinds* of evils. Nonetheless, the love of money is exposed as the root of many of our problems, not pride. Jesus speaks to the same power of avarice when he famously says, "You cannot serve God and money" (Matthew 6:24). Could it be the perverse nature of pride itself to (pridefully) assert that it alone must be the cause of all our other problems? It is just like pride to insist that if it cannot be the best, then it will instead be the worst—but at least be first in *something*. As Milton made Lucifer say, "Better to reign in hell than serve in heaven."

If we end up claiming that pride is the root of all other sins, if we define pride as being assertive about what is best for us, we will tend to think of the Christian path, following Jesus, as putting ourselves down. We may even be tempted (like Lucifer) to choose to reign in hell instead. But Jesus tells us he has come to offer life and life abundantly; we are promised fullness of joy, love, peace, freedom—all the things that are totally the opposite of self-hate.

Christians are, of course, called upon to love others, serve others, remember that "it is more blessed to give than to receive" (Acts 20:35)—but if we understand humility as putting ourselves down, or putting ourselves to one side, then how can "I" put "myself" to one side, without putting "I" and "myself" back in the center, as the hero who put "I" and "myself" to one side?

It is a vicious cycle and a kind of Orwellian "double-think" to this path of attempting to follow Jesus that (again) a good Freudian analyst would have a field day with. "I" exist, and therefore if "I" am worshiping God alone, and putting God at the center of everything, am "I" not to be congratulated? Does this make Christians who are successful at putting themselves down in this way less obvious but still real "Uriah Heeps"?

A woman went up to a preacher after a worship service and told him that she had not sinned for ten years. The minister replied after a moment's thought, "You must be rather proud about that." To which the womanly artlessly responded, "Yes, I am actually."

Is pride actually then the center of all our difficulties? It depends how you define *pride*. If by *pride*, you mean the "selfish self," then yes, I think pride is the center of all our difficulties or, rather, Jesus does. It is not by accident that in these seven callings from Jesus to follow him, he twice tells each of us to take up our cross. It is not by accident that the famous hinge point of Mark's Gospel, chapter 8, is all about the disciples realizing not only that Jesus must die (he is that kind of Messiah) but also that to follow him they must die to themselves (they are to be those sort of disciples).

But does this mean that to be a Christian is to put yourself down? No, although it does mean to deny yourself. To understand the difference, we will need to remember who we were as well as who we are. Before the Fall, in the garden of Eden, Adam and Eve were still "selves." Adam was an "I," an individual, made perfect, and in perfect relation to God as his Creator. Adam's self was fully "self-*ing*," fully self-*ed*, yet he was not self-*ish* in the sense that we use the word now. His self was fully in communion with God. His self was made in the image of God, with God as the ruler, and Adam as the under-ruler, the vice-regent, over the garden as God's representative (his image). This self was not sinful; it was fully how the self should be.

> That sinful, selfish, wounded and ruined, wounding and ruining self has to go.

After the Fall, however, when Adam and Eve were expelled from the garden, the self took on a new role. Now the self became selfish; it was no longer acting under God's rule, under his sway, or as his representative. Every part of the image is now tainted, though the created self is still there. When we act as our selves, we are selfish; it is unavoidable, for anyone who is not fully submitted to God is using the self for itself and not for God and others—and that is "selfish."

So when Jesus says, "Come after me, take up your cross, deny yourself," he is not saying, "Put yourself down." To be a Christian does mean fully to follow Jesus and put him first and above all, and at the very center. But if we don't grasp who we originally were as created and are now as fallen human beings (in our "selves"), we will misunderstand what Jesus is saying here about denying the self to be simply a way of putting ourselves down, keeping ourselves down. What Jesus is saying is that the selfish self must die: the sick self, the wounded self, the hurting self, the unreal self, the fake self.

If this is pride, then it is the root of all sin. We have a mask (a metaphorical fig leaf), all of us, a selfish self, a self covering up the original and now marred, ruining the true made-in-God's-image self. It's a mask that takes that original self, the one that could rightly be "self-*ed*"—expressed, formed, articulated, energized, fulfilled—and makes it self-*ish*. Jesus is saying, "Kill that self; kill that fake self. For far too long it has dominated you and twisted you. It has locked you up and ruined you. It has to go. You have to bring it out into the open and let it wither in the light of truth and love. That sinful, selfish, wounded and ruined, wounding and ruining self has to go. Deny it; then you—your real, original self—come follow me."

It's another form of *metanoia*, changing your mind, repenting in the right sense of the word, and then believing in the *mysterion* of the gospel, following Jesus as his disciple.

Jesus' fifth "I Am" statement in John's Gospel underlines the beauty and freedom of our Master calling us to deny this torturous self to follow him in our true, created-by-him selves. It comes in the middle of the story about Lazarus, who died, and Jesus, who seemed to wait until he died before he went to help. There he is, with Lazarus already dead and buried four days, and Martha meets him and says that if Jesus had been there, Lazarus would not have died.

Jesus will bring Lazarus back to life, a miracle intended to teach us that Jesus has literal and physical power over death and life. Lazarus, though, will eventually die again. What would that have been like? To have died once and then to face it again? Lazarus's miracle is not just a miracle about the resurrection in a physical sense but also about the resurrection in a spiritual sense, the new birth, the dying to self, denying self, the "taking up your cross." The one is about the other, for the one leads to the other, and is the fruit of the other. As we each take up our cross, we are getting ready for a physical death and then a physical resurrection.

So Jesus says, "Your brother will rise again," meaning that he is about to bring him physically back to life. Martha replies with the pious faith of her time, saying that she knows that he will rise again on the last day. But Jesus has something else in mind: not only a coming back to life now but also a message about who he is ("I Am") and what that means for those who follow him and believe him:

> Martha said to Jesus, "Lord, if you had been here, my brother would not have died. But even now I know that whatever you ask from God, God will give you." Jesus said to her, "Your brother will rise again." Martha said to him, "I know that he will rise again in the resurrection on the last day." Jesus said to her, "I am the resurrection and the life. Whoever believes in me, though he die, yet shall he live, and everyone who lives and believes in me shall never die. Do you believe this?" She said to him, "Yes, Lord; I believe that you are the Christ, the Son of God, who is coming into the world." (John 11:21-27)

"I am the resurrection and the life." What a statement! Jesus is! He does not just give resurrection and life; he *is* the resurrection and the life. Joined to that, believing in that, believing in him, though we die yet shall we live and living and believing shall never die. Our selves are put back in touch with the

source of life and resurrection (no, with Life and Resurrection *himself*), and so the selfish self has died, and we (our true selves, now believing in Jesus, following him) will never die.

WHO YOU WERE MEANT TO BE

In a sense, being humble is simply being who you were meant to be. People often say that humility is not thinking less of yourself but rather thinking of yourself less—and there is a lot of truth to that statement. I have used it myself at times to explain how humility is not about putting yourself down. Yes, humility is not about believing worse things about yourself, and yes, humility does involve thinking of yourself less, and instead thinking of other people more, and God above all. But how do we get there? How do we have this change to thinking less about ourselves and more about other people and, most of all, more about God? And how do we maintain that without being proud that we are thinking of ourselves less?

In some ways, the fifth of seven of Jesus' signs in John's Gospel tells us about this and helps us with this idea of being who you were meant to be. Each of the signs has an evangelistic purpose: they are intended (as John tells us) "that you may believe that Jesus is the Christ, the Son of God, and that by believing you may have life in his name" (John 20:31). They are evangelistic in that the signs help us believe in Jesus, but they are not *merely* evangelistic if that means just helping people to believe for the first time. They help us believe who Jesus is, to have confidence in Jesus as the Christ and as the Son of God. They are not simply tools or techniques for marketing Jesus; they are meant to show Jesus as who he is.

This issue of identity is very much at the heart of the fifth sign. It is the famous account of Jesus walking on the water, and to arrive at the point about how it underlines Jesus' identity, we need to read the story again, and then put it in its context.

> When evening came, his disciples went down to the sea, got into a boat, and started across the sea to Capernaum. It was now dark, and Jesus had not yet come to them. The sea became rough because a strong wind was blowing. When they had rowed about three or four miles, they saw Jesus walking on the sea and coming near the boat, and they were frightened. But he said to them, "It is I; do not be afraid." Then they were glad to take him into the boat, and immediately the boat was at the land to which they were going. (John 6:16-21)

In context Jesus reveals here who he is, and in recognizing his identity it helps us (again) with our sense of identity—our "being who we were meant to be." When Jesus says, "Do not be afraid," he begins that sentence with the phrase that translates into English as, "It is I." This is a statement that in Greek (*Ego Eimi*) can also be translated "I Am." Indeed, in context that phrase is used that way several times after this sign to emphasize that Jesus may not just have been saying, "Don't worry; it's me! Your friend Jesus! See? I'm not a weird ghost; it's me—Jesus!" But he may also be saying, "Don't be afraid; I AM," referring to the great proclamation of "I AM" of God Himself in the Old Testament (Exodus 3:14). That is, Jesus, by walking on the water, is not only showing that he is astonishingly, out-of-this-world powerful but also saying that by doing this act of breaking the normal bounds of the created order (walking on water), he is revealing to us and the disciples "I AM." He is showing his divinity.

And in context of this sign, the fifth of the seven in John's Gospel, Jesus goes on to deliberately teach that he is the "I AM" (*Ego Eimi*, the "I AM who I AM," Exodus 3:14) in John 6:35, 8:24, and then finally and most controversially in John 8:58. There at the end of this developing teaching about his identity, finally, "Jesus said to them, 'Truly, truly, I say to you, before Abraham was, I am.'" And just so we hear the radical nature of what Jesus says there, we are told about how his original hearers understood immediately: they picked up stones to throw at him for what they perceived to be blasphemy, that Jesus, whom they considered merely another human, was claiming equality with God (John 8:59).

Now what does this have to do with humility, with taking up our crosses and following Jesus—that great command to follow him, to deny ourselves, which we are looking at this "Friday," repeated from "Thursday," also saying, "Take up your cross" then too? What it is telling us is that, again, this self has become warped into what we commonly call a "selfish" self, and must worship him (not us) as the "I AM." That what we are to do is to "be who we were meant to be." It is a case of not only thinking about ourselves less but also recognizing who he is—and therefore who we are not, and who we are in relation to him. It is being who we were made to be.

The biblical notions of humility, pride, taking up our crosses, and denying ourselves all revolve around the basic truth that we, in our "I" state, are constantly trying to make our "I" the "I AM." We are playing at God: that is the very nature of pride. Pride, biblically, is not thinking highly of yourself. It is not thinking that you are better than you really are at tennis, nor is it just thinking about yourself too much and not being sufficiently concerned with other people and their achievements. It is true that a humble person, a person who has denied himself and taken up his cross, is someone who thinks about other people and, most of all and above all, about God. This means that this person can take delight in other people, in their achievements, and not feel jealous or annoyed when they are not in the spotlight. This is all true, but it is more the result than the essence, more the fruit than the root, of pride, and of humility, which is its opposite.

> Our confusion about who we are and where we come from and what we are meant to be is solved only as we are "lost in wonder, love, and praise."

What we are talking about when we say "take up your cross" is that we are identifying ourselves with Jesus, who took up his cross. When we say "deny yourself," it means that we are denying that the self is the great "I AM"; instead, we are looking at Jesus (who changed water into wine, walked on water, rose from the dead; the Creator; the great "I AM"). We are looking at Jesus and saying he is the "I."

This is what it means in the words of the great hymn to be "lost in wonder, love, and praise."

> Love divine, all loves excelling,
> Joy of heaven to earth come down;
> Fix in us thy humble dwelling;
> All thy faithful mercies crown!
> Jesus, Thou art all compassion,
> Pure unbounded love Thou art;
> Visit us with Thy salvation;
> Enter every trembling heart.[4]

He fixes in us his humble dwelling. Who he is, is revealed in us, combined with us, connected with us, entered into us, bound to us; all his mercies, compassion, and love. And so at the end of this process of discipleship in this world:

> Finish, then, Thy new creation;
> Pure and spotless let us be.
> Let us see Thy great salvation
> Perfectly restored in thee;
> Changed from glory into glory,
> Till in heaven we take our place,
> Till we cast our crowns before Thee,
> Lost in wonder, love, and praise.[5]

We are the New Creation, and in the end, on the final day, and the goal to which by faith we are advancing gradually now, we will be perfectly restored in Jesus, in heaven. We will cast our crowns—any of our achievements, even those done in his name and for him and in his power—before him, and in that famous phrase, then we will be "lost in wonder, love, and praise."

Who loses themselves to find themselves? Who denies themselves to fulfill themselves? Who kills themselves (takes up their crosses) to live as themselves? Who? Christians, that's who; disciples: people who have got it, understood it, embraced it, that the great "I AM" is not our individual "I" but Jesus.

It is then truly and actually all about Jesus. Our confusion about who we are and where we come from and what we are meant to be is solved only as we are "lost in wonder, love, and praise." It is not solved by psychoanalysis on its own, though I am sure that counseling and therapy can be used by God. The end point, the goal, is not to "discover" myself but to surrender myself to him, to his *self*. We need not to "find ourselves" but to "lose ourselves." And the ultimate finding of our self is not in the journey to the self, or taking care of the self, or the loving of the self, but the ultimate and only true finding of the self is in the losing of the self in worship of Jesus as "I Am."

"I Am; do not be afraid."

"It is I; do not be afraid."

And so we come to the fifth of the seven letters of Jesus to the churches in Asia, this time to Sardis. Sardis, and Jesus' word to it, in many ways represents the matter of pride and the importance of humility in the spiritual life and in being revitalized, this matter that we have been considering today, this "Friday."

> To the angel of the church in Sardis write: These are
> the words of him who holds the seven spirits of God

and the seven stars. I know your deeds; you have a reputation of being alive, but you are dead. Wake up! Strengthen what remains and is about to die, for I have found your deeds unfinished in the sight of my God. Remember, therefore, what you received and heard; hold it fast, and repent. But if you do not wake up, I will come like a thief, and you will not know at what time I will come to you. Yet you have a few people in Sardis who have not soiled their clothes. They will walk with me, dressed in white, for they are worthy. The one who is victorious will, like them, be dressed in white. I will never blot out the name of that person from the book of life, but will acknowledge that name before my Father and his angels. Whoever has ears, let them hear what the Spirit says to the churches. (Revelation 3:1-6 NIV)

That pride comes before the fall is a well-known proverb, and the letter to the church of Sardis stands as an illustration of that truth. Sardis itself was a city with claims to ancient glory. It had in times gone by been the capital of various ancient empires. It was, in particular, a rock citadel of unusual and impressive strength. The citadel was situated atop a large hill with sheer precipices that barred ascent to the city by all points save one. This narrow ascent from the south was easily fortified. And as such, this rock citadel prided itself on being impregnable.

This pride came before its fall. Several times in its history it had, in fact, caved in to the pressure of foreign invaders. Most famously, it fell to a siege when an army encamped outside its sheer rock-face walls detailed a sole climber up the mountain, who opened the gates from inside. It seems clear from the contemporary accounts that such a victory against Sardis was only achieved by the sleepiness of the inhabitants. They thought no one could take their city, and they hardly even bothered to guard the gates. You can find this story in the work of ancient historian Herodotus, embellished to some extent, no doubt, but nonetheless a story that became proverbial for the city of Sardis.[6]

What's more, the very substance of the seemingly impregnable rock walls had been devastated just a few years before this letter from Jesus. In AD 17, there was a stunningly catastrophic earthquake, which hit Sardis hardest of all. The rock on which the city perched is made of crumbly material, and the earthquake devastated a large portion of this city. Pliny, another ancient historian, writes about it and records how an enormous amount of financial relief was channeled toward Sardis from the Emperor Tiberius as a result. Sardis, seemingly impregnable, actually had lamely capitulated to a whole series of foreign invaders and was perched atop an unstable foundation. Now Sardis is just a village, and the top of the hill, which held the citadel, is about a third the size because of the earthquakes and other subsequent erosion of the precarious material of which it is made.

And the church, commonly enough, had taken on some of the characteristics of its environment. It too was sleepy. It too had a reputation of being alive. It too would be defeated if it did not wake up and guard the gates against a thief in the night. It too was proud; it too was in danger of a fall.

"Of course," someone says, "this has no relevance to the contemporary religious scene in which we find ourselves. Of course not. We never hear of a televangelist with a private plane who receives money for it from paupers. And even if we did, it would be something for others to deal with. After all, we're quite nice; we do the right thing; we go about our business with God and with people in as kind a way as we can. We wear our smile even if inside we are burning with anger or in turmoil of fear. We do good, nonetheless, and we look good to others, and surely this is what is really all that is required of us from God. No one could say we are in any kind of desperate need morally. We're better than a lot of other people. And surely if we look good and seem good, then this is strong enough to withstand the storms of life, the invasion of the enemy. Our spiritual citadel is pretty impressive, don't you think?"

"I know your deeds" the reply comes. *"You have a reputation of being alive, but you are dead. Wake up!"* This mixed metaphor that runs throughout the passage is not to confuse us. The Lord Jesus is expressing himself so as to sidestep the defense of our external appearance. He is ringing the changes metaphorically to sound the alarm about the condition of looking good but not actually being good. The cry "Wake up!" may, perhaps, have actually been a historic last-minute reminder to the city before it fell to the foreign invaders. Here Jesus is issuing it in a new context. *There is a climber ascending your fortress; it appears you are safe; you are not; arouse yourself, wake up!* They were dead asleep, and they needed to be aroused by this alarm bell.

What the letter is written to teach us, then, is this: "Looking good is not the same as being good." We may (proudly) feel pretty good about where we are, who we are, and what we are doing, but Jesus says that is very different from actually being in the right place with him, and in life. The letter describes the *appearance*, the *problem*, and the *solution*.

The Appearance

Verse 1: "To the angel of the church in Sardis write: These are the words of him who holds the seven spirits of God and the seven stars. I know your deeds; you have a reputation of being alive, but you are dead." That their deeds are merely reputation and not reality, an appearance but not substance, is emphasized by the way this letter introduces the one whose words it records: holding the seven spirits and the seven stars.

The "seven spirits" are before the "throne" of God (Revelation 1:4). Justin Martyr, an early Christian apologist, explains the different roles for the Holy Spirit as predicted in Isaiah 11:2.[7] The seven spirits are characteristics of the one Holy Spirit, who is therefore more than sufficient to meet the needs of each of the seven churches of these letters in Revelation 2–3, including Sardis, so that the church there has no need for pretending to have a reputation of being alive. If this interpretation is right—that the "seven spirits" refer to the work of the one Holy Spirit—the text assumes a thoroughly trinitarian view of God to counteract our human tendency to only pretend to do what God wants. Jesus "holds" the "seven spirits" (verse 1), implying an interrelationship of the Spirit with Jesus as God. At the same time, Jesus also calls the Father God "my God" (verse 2). So this Jesus—the Lord Jesus of majestic fire and authority as described in Revelation again and again, in the center of the throne of heaven, and so on—is modeling for us the essential submission found in the Trinity, not merely as an appearance but as a joyful reality. Jesus willingly, not begrudgingly or only apparently, submits to his Father God while remaining fully and equally God himself.

The "seven stars" are the seven angels of the churches (see Revelation 1:20). Who these angels were is up for debate, but I lean toward the ancient, if unfashionable, view that they were the gospel messengers of the churches, that is, the pastors. It would make sense for the letter to be written to them and then be read out to the churches. Jesus "holds" them also, and so to his words spoken through them we are not only to appear to listen but also to really pay attention.

All of this introduction to the letter, then, is best approached from the issue of reputation or mere appearance that is at the heart of the passage. Their deeds made them look good. The reality was otherwise, and the message to their messenger, from the real and not just apparent Trinity—Father, Son, and Holy Spirit—was about to reveal the problem.

THE PROBLEM

What was wrong? Their deeds were "unfinished" (verse 2). They had forgotten the message and so needed to "remember, therefore, what you have received and heard; hold it fast, and repent" (verse 3).

Good deeds can hide a bad heart. They were not being persecuted, unlike their fellow Christians in other cities in Asia.

They were not giving way to heresy. They were not inactive. They were not asleep because they were being passive or lazy. They were *doing* a lot. But they held in extreme form a tendency of all of these churches in Asia in one way or another. They were all slipping from the original grasping of the message of grace to a form of legalistic righteousness. Such legalistic "deeds" can never be complete in the sight of God. They needed to remember what they had originally heard, *hold it fast*, and turn back to the purity of the gospel.

I come across this all the time. I say to someone, "What you need is to believe in Jesus alone and be saved." They come back and say, "I know I need to be more religious." Not what I'm talking about. I say grace; they think deeds. I say faith; they think works. I say church; they think moral guilt. I say God, they think, *Oh no. More moral judgments.* The trouble with the church at Sardis was that the people were resting on their deeds. They thought these were enough. They were proud of their deeds, much like the city was proud of its great fortress.

> The person relying on Jesus alone for his or her justification says, "I cannot, but with God's strength in my weakness, I am strong, and now I can."

But such a city of deeds had a terrible weakness. It was not sufficient; it would fall. Our deeds cannot be complete in the sight of God. We may have a reputation among our friends for being holy, but God knows better. And so do we! It is an appearance, but it is not the reality. Who can say that their deeds are complete in the sight of God? What arrogance! What pride! What a great fall there will be unless we wake up and see the problem.

You may be thinking, *I've heard this before.* Or *I've heard about "faith and believing in Jesus."* Or *I'll try to do better.*

But there is a reality, a gospel reality to the seven spirits of God, to the trinitarian nature of God, to his holiness and greatness and power, to the message of the gospel. And believing in Jesus is not merely about doing more. We think to ourselves: *Look, God, I'm doing my bit. Why don't you come along and do yours, sort this problem out for me?* But that is the problem: salvation is not half me and half God. It's fully God and nothing of me. It is a deep humility utterly foreign to the Sardis spirit.

The person who is relying on his or her incomplete deeds for favor with God says something like this: "All I need to do is work on this more, do this better." The person who is relying on Jesus alone for his or her justification before God says, "I cannot, but with God's strength in my weakness, I am strong, and now I can." The people trusting their works are stuck; their works are never finished. The people trusting their works are guilty; their works are never over. The people trusting their works have activities that are never complete because they are always digging up the root again to see if they've managed to make it perfect. Of course they haven't made it perfect! How could deeds be perfect in the sight of God?

THE SOLUTION

Verse 3: "Remember." Verse 4: "Yet you have a few people in Sardis who have not soiled their clothes. They will walk with me, dressed in white, for they are worthy." Verse 5: "I will never blot out the name of that person from the book of life." They are to remember what they heard—the message of the gospel—and move back into line with that. This message of the gospel is what will cause them to wear pure clothes and ensure that their names are never erased from the book of life. Interestingly enough, Sardis was an early center of wool dyeing. Being "dressed in white" may have had special resonance with them. Also, every Roman triumphal procession paraded the victors in white garments. The symbolism is one of purity and victory. They are worthy.

The "book of life" is an Old Testament reference and one with ancient civic overtones. When Moses prayed that the people of God would be spared God's judgment, he asked that instead his name be blotted out of the book of life (Exodus 32:32). In ancient society there was a practice of keeping a civic roll of citizens. It is like the electoral role of heaven. Their names would never be erased—the word is the Greek word for the process of removing someone from the citizenship roster of a city's list—never erased from the book of life, eternal life in heaven.

The solution, then, is a real, authentic, radical, genuine relationship with Jesus. This is what they are to remember. This is what caused them to be justified, worthy even in the sight of God. This is what ensures their permanent status in heaven. This is the historic, biblical doctrine of "justification by faith alone." Faith—that is a personal trust in Jesus as you would trust a good friend. Justification—that is the legal status of being acquitted as guiltless. Alone—that is, no other moral, religious, or human effort can secure it. This justification by faith alone is what secures the personal commitment from Jesus never to blot us out of the book of life, to be those who "walk with" him through life and eternity and to be worthy, dressed purely. We are good before God; our status is not just guiltless but also righteous because of what Jesus has done on the cross. It is imputed to us, his righteousness, that is, reckoned to us and covering over us, so that our great and many moral failings are no longer a barrier. They are covered by Christ's great and final sacrifice. And I'm not talking about being more religious.

Looking good is not the same as being good. The appearance: a reputation of life. The problem: a reality of death. The solution: a relationship with Jesus. Or we could say that Sardis had a name, they had fame, but they were lame! Christians who trust the biblical gospel, though, have a relationship, a righteousness, and a reward.

The church at Sardis had been influenced by the culture in which it was placed. It too had grown proud and sleepy, like the proud and sleepy people of the seemingly impregnable fortress of Sardis. What is it about our culture, our city, our region that subconsciously influences our attitude toward religion, church, and God? Do we tend to interpret all messages from the angels of God's churches as species of moral pragmatism? Do we tend to assume that our citizenship in heaven must be secure because of where we were born? Do we tend to think that our understanding of the gospel must be accurate because, after all, we did quite well on our academic test scores? What deeds are we relying on? None are complete in the sight of God. Only faith in Christ will save us. Wake up! The alarm in the house has gone off. There is a thief of moral pride trying to enter the citadel of your heart. Will you get up and repudiate it in favor of trusting in Jesus? Or will you turn over in bed to get another forty winks?

So the letter of Sardis is a powerful antidote to the "Sardis spirit," the spirit of pride, rather than—the opposite—taking up our crosses and following Jesus. Rather than resting our "I" in the great "I AM," rather than not being afraid because of the "I AM" revealed as the Creator, walking on water, the Resurrection and Life, we hide ourselves, our little "I," playing at god, when God comes calling us to follow him. But if we will, by his Spirit, respond to his call to follow him, then we will move out of the small-minded, human-level, insecure world of puny "I," to the greatness of a real connection to the Creator, the Redeemer, the Lord of All, the great "I AM."

"If my people who are called by my name humble themselves, and pray and seek my face and turn from their wicked ways, then I will hear from heaven and will forgive their sin and heal their land" (2 Chronicles 7:14). Time to turn from ourselves to find ourselves in losing ourselves, in following him.

A Day for Greatness

Jesus said to him, "If you would be perfect, go, sell what you possess and give to the poor, and you will have treasure in heaven; and come, follow me."

—*Matthew 19:21*

No one really knows for sure why the first Christian monks appeared. One of the best explanations is that as the church became more successful and was established in the late Roman Empire after Constantine, there was a natural feeling among some that it was time to return to an original, simpler life. As the church became more popular, there were no longer even possible persecutions against the church, and as the church grew wealthier, there were people who felt that something pure, innocent, and good had been lost. Another explanation for the beginning of the first monks is that the late Roman Empire was influenced by various "mystery" religions from the East, and that monks and other guru-like individuals were popular forms of piety.

Whatever the reason, informally at first, and only much later in an institutional way, some radical individuals began to separate themselves from the normal run of society, go off into the desert in Syria and Egypt, and start to behave in ways that we think of as renouncing the world, doing without possessions. There was very little of a community nature to this movement at first but rather individual, particular "holy" people. Strangely, these radical disciples started to gain a lot of power and influence, because their reputation for holiness spread, and people came from a long way away to ask them questions. There were biblical precedents for such early monastic behavior, as people appealed to the Nazirite vow of the Old Testament or the behavior of John the Baptist if some went considerably beyond these ideals. Anthony the Great is thought to be the father of monasticism, though the movement existed before him. Perhaps the strangest early monastic figure was Simeon Stylites, who became famous for spending thirty-seven years on top of a pillar. Children would bring him simple bread and food, and it is said that at one point his pillar extended to fifteen meters (around fifty feet) high. People would come to ask him advice; he would preach and perform his regular devotions on top of this pillar. He died there.

Later in the history of monasticism, and perhaps to curb the extremes of the movement—some of those following the early exalted heroes were of less sane a temperament than the reportedly otherwise sensible Simeon—there emerged particular rules, ways of behaving under strict discipline within a community, or a "monastery." The most famous of these rules is the rule of Benedict, from which we have the common figure of the Benedictine monk still today.

Are all Christians to renounce money? Is money inherently evil, possessions necessarily bad, and a "secular" career inevitably a distraction from the Christian life? Or, if it is permissible to be a Christian and earn money and own possessions, can you only be a truly superlative Christian if you follow the example of the early monastic movement, or indeed if you "sell what you possess and give to the poor." Is this the only way to have "treasure in heaven"?

> Generosity is the rule. The point of money is that it is not the end but the means—and a powerful means, a powerful tool.

Taken as a whole, the Bible's attitude to money is basically that money is a powerful means, a tool to be used wisely and carefully for God and his kingdom. But because it is such a powerful tool, it has especially dangerous temptations connected to it. So money is not the root of all evil, but the *love* of money is the root of all kinds of evil. Job, in the Old Testament, is a very wealthy man, and his wealth is not against his piety, but rather expresses his piety, and when he has been through his suffering, his wealth is returned to him with even more added. Paul does not urge the Christians to give up all their money, but rather to share generously with those in need. It is true that some among the early Christian communities in Acts sold their possessions, houses, and fields and gave to those in need so that there were no poor among them, but the very fact that they sold their houses and fields tells us that they had houses and fields to sell. When a couple is severely disciplined for misbehavior with regard to their possessions, it is not because they did not sell their property; it is because they lied about how much money they got. They were disciplined for deception, not materialism; the field was theirs; they could do with it as they pleased.

Generosity is the rule, not poverty as such. For, as some joker has quipped, if money was itself evil, it would do no good to the poor to give it to them. The point of money is that it is not the end but the means—and a powerful means, a powerful tool, and as such a powerful tool, it has particular dangers. It is easy to "love" money.

The person in Jesus' story in Matthew's Gospel who is commanded by Jesus to sell all his possessions is an idolater. He has kept all the rules (or he thinks he has), but what he lacks is the ability, the desire, to actually follow Jesus. He is not following God; he is following money. So then it makes no difference, in a sense, whether he "keeps all the rules" or not, because the whole aim of the rules is that he would be following God. That he will not do. He has an idol, and when Jesus tells him to get rid of his money and give to the poor, the key point of the sentence is the last: "And come, follow me." These possessions are stopping the man from following Jesus.

That is why it is so hard, as Jesus will go on to explain, for the rich to enter the kingdom of God. Money is a powerful tool, and it is easy to become fascinated by the tool rather than by the goal. The rich man is like a carpenter so fixated with his latest power tool that he no longer is building houses; he's just

144

playing with the tool. He needs to get back to building houses; he needs to get back to following God, to come and follow Jesus. There are times when money does become an idol, and the only thing to do is apply the radical surgery that Jesus supplies here: get rid of it, and then come, follow Jesus.

But it's not just money.

SERVE

As intoxicating as money can be for some people, if not more addictive is the drug of power, influence, fame, and ambition. This series of words, each echoing a desire in the human heart for "greatness" in the sense of an idolatry, are particularly difficult issues to surmount. Jesus even met these problems among his own disciples, people who had already begun to follow him. For unlike gross idolization of money, ambition can be covered up by extreme piety; we can be ambitious for God, ambitious for church, ambitious to win souls to follow Jesus. And as these are all worthy ambitions, it can be hard at times to discern whether we are actually using these ambitions to attain our core ambition, which is an ambition to be great. We are simply using the Christian religion as a means to this other end.

In Mark 10:35-52, James and John ask Jesus to do for them whatever they ask. Immediately we have a problem! Mayday! This is the wrong way around; you do not go up to Jesus to ask him to do for you whatever you ask. There is that demon pride. There is the demon selfishness. But what is this demon leading John and James to want? What is their ambition?

Soon it becomes clear; what they want is glory, fame, greatness. They ask Jesus for one of them to sit at his left and the other at his right when Jesus comes to glory. (How James and John, so caught up with ambitious desire for greatness, would be able to decide which of them got to sit on the right, and which on the left, I am still unclear.) Jesus is gracious with them. For they do not really understand what they are asking. Jesus' glory is revealed at the cross, so to sit at his right and left means to be crucified with him. "Can you drink the cup that I drink, or be baptized with the baptism I am baptized with?" (v. 38 NIV). They have no doubts that they are perfectly capable of this, thinking perhaps it is their kind of greatness that the cup and baptism represent, rather than the whipping, the beating, and the crucifixion.

Of course, when the other disciples hear about this request of James and John, they are incensed. Why should *they* get to sit at Jesus' right and Jesus' left? What about us? Ambition and a desire for greatness have produced what they nearly always produce: division. Someone wants to be first; the other people don't want to be left out; inevitably you have tension. So Jesus calls them together and teaches them about greatness:

> You know that those who are considered rulers of the Gentiles lord it over them, and their great ones exercise authority over them. But it shall not be so among you. But whoever would be great among you must be your servant, and whoever would be first among you must be slave of all. For even the Son of Man came not to be served but to serve, and to give his life as a ransom for many (Mark 10:42-45).

146

Jesus does not tell them not to want to be great. He tells them that their idea of greatness is distorted. They think of greatness the same way that the rulers of the Gentiles think of greatness. Greatness is the ability to "lord it over" other people, to be in charge, to exercise authority over others. Jesus says that's not greatness at all; real greatness is actually being the servant, and the very first is the servant of everyone. All Christian leadership takes its cue, its instructions, and its mandate from these words. Leaders are to be servants; the first leader is to be the servant of all. Jesus himself is the ultimate example of this: his whole reason for coming to earth, for being born as a man, and dying for us, was not to be served but to serve and die to ransom many.

It is instructive, then, that perhaps the greatest English-speaking evangelist of all time took as his mandate these words of Jesus. His motto was "servant of all." George Whitefield, the English evangelist, sometimes called "the great itinerant," traveled across the Atlantic many times, preached thousands upon thousands of sermons to tens of thousands of people, in an age without modern modes of transport, communication, or even amplification. He was said to have been able to communicate clearly to thirty thousand people outside, without (of course) the aid of a microphone. He had a simple, direct style, with great oratory, not just talking about David or Paul, but becoming, in a sense, Paul and David, as people watched and listened to his preaching.

But Whitefield was not always so exalted. At Oxford he was not part of the elevated group, but rather a more servant-like class, and from those days, it seems, he learned the value of serving. He took the art with him wherever he went. He was "servant of all." It is not easy to maintain that spirit in the midst of fame and adulation, and no doubt Whitefield did not always perfectly achieve it, but there was a sense in which, his biographers tend to confirm, Whitefield, while so charismatic a personality and such a strong leader, was not out to dominate other people. He was there to lift up other people, to serve them with what was best for them, to come alongside and build up. He was the consummate publicist, no doubt, writing scores upon scores of letters to his contacts, promoting the work in which he was involved. He had a massive auditorium built as his base in London. There was nothing retiring about Whitefield. But his greatness was not lording it over others, but rather serving others.

We see another, and very different, example of this serving kind of greatness in the sixth of Jesus' seven signs in John's Gospel. This man was not famous, not "great," not traveling far and wide and becoming well-known; he was simply a "man blind from birth":

> As he passed by, he saw a man blind from birth. And his disciples asked him, "Rabbi, who sinned, this man or his parents, that he was born blind?" Jesus answered, "It was not that this man sinned, or his parents, but that the works of God might be displayed in him. We must work the works of him who sent me while it is day; night is coming, when no one can work. As long as I am in the world, I am the light of the world." Having said these things, he spit on the ground and made mud with the saliva. Then he anointed the man's eyes

with the mud and said to him, "Go, wash in the pool of Siloam" (which means Sent). So he went and washed and came back seeing. (John 9:1-7)

This man born blind is not even given a name here, though I am sure his name is known to the One who knows all. The question that the disciples ask Jesus about why he is born blind, reflects theological discussion and assumptions at the time. Because suffering was thought to be a result of sin, if someone was born with such a painful and harmful problem, then it must be the sin of either the individual or of his or her parents. Either answer presents problems, especially as this person has had his blindness since he was born. What is the answer?

The answer is neither. It is not the man's or his parents' sin that caused this. There is not a direct one-to-one correlation between personal sin and personal suffering, at least not always. Suffering is the fruit of sin, generally speaking, but the sin of the world in rebellion against God has produced a situation where the whole world is out of joint, and horrible things happen to people who have done nothing themselves to deserve it.

It was not his sin; it was not his parents' sin. But then why the blindness? The sinful rebellion of all of humanity and the resulting suffering is used by God to reveal Jesus. This happened "that the works of God might be displayed in him."

Sometimes the very worst

> Greatness in the Bible is serving a higher purpose. It is connecting ourselves with the great stream of reality and life and truth (and God).

things happen to us, are inflicted upon us, so that the works of God might be displayed in us. That Jesus might be shown through us. Perhaps you have a son or daughter who has been ill since birth. Whose fault is that? Is it yours? Is it the child's fault? Has he or she done something wrong to deserve this affliction? Why does this happen to you when other families, perhaps some families who are less devoted to God than you, less moral than you, have children who are thriving? "That the works of God might be displayed in him." In this man's case that was an immediate healing from the touch of Jesus. In some of our cases, it is a spiritual healing that will lead to a physical healing in the resurrection to come. The man born blind is made to see as an example of Jesus being the light of the world. He was a servant to a higher purpose.

Greatness in the Bible is serving this higher purpose. It is connecting ourselves with the great stream of reality and life and truth (and God), so that we are pointing to and a part of the Greatness. "Your God is too small," as the Bible translator J. B. Phillips would say. Not only is our God too small but also our concept of greatness is too small. We want greatness and have ambition for it, but because we do not serve, we will never get it. The man or woman who achieves greatness through lording it over others rarely goes down in history as a truly great man or woman. It is the man or woman with a great purpose, one beyond himself or herself, beyond the small-mindedness of the here and now, to the eternal stream of justice, mercy, compassion, truth, and God. That is Greatness with a capital G.

In the relaunch of the BBC science fiction show *Doctor*

Who, one of the key ideas that is repeated is this sense of the enormity of the universe, of space and time. The TARDIS, the rather strange bigger-on-the-inside-than-the-outside space-ship that the "Doctor" travels in, has a vortex in its central core, which shows a part of the mystery of space and time through which the TARDIS is able to travel. To peer into this vortex can render you mad. It can destroy you. It is so immense that it can blow your mind.

If the universe, in some way or other, is like that, what is the Creator of the universe like? The vision of Isaiah perhaps comes closest in the Bible to describing the pure immensity of God:

> In the year that King Uzziah died I saw the Lord sitting upon a throne, high and lifted up; and the train of his robe filled the temple. Above him stood the seraphim. Each had six wings: with two he covered his face, and with two he covered his feet, and with two he flew. And one called to another and said: "Holy, holy, holy is the LORD of hosts; the whole earth is full of his glory." (Isaiah 6:1-3)

What is God like if the universe is so immense, powerful, and indescribably great? Answer: greater by far. And his greatness by far is not *only* in his immensity and power and might (Lord of Hosts) but also, and most particularly, in his holiness: "Holy, holy, holy, is the LORD of hosts." His holiness three times repeated is a way of saying that he is not just holy, not just very holy, but utterly pure and good and blindingly righteous, separate, distinct, above all in the might of his morality, and in the clarity of his ethical essence. This God is the One we are to serve if we are to be truly great.

Isaiah's commission is an unenviable one: go and tell these people, but they won't listen (Isaiah 6:9). Still, he was connected to the source of all goodness and greatness himself, and in serving that person (not just purpose), he achieved a genuine greatness.

GIVE

Generosity at every level, not just the financial but the generosity of soul that includes the giving of the self in service of others, cannot really genuinely occur without a compelling vision of the Other, of who God is, of who Jesus is. Someone can give away much but do so in bitterness of soul or spirit; someone can serve but do so as a slave, with a slave spirit, unwilling, and burdened by the activity. There are many instances of people giving, and serving, without a true vision of God and of Jesus, without a sense of the Other and their involvement with him, but such giving, and such serving, tends by its very nature to be done with a sense of loss. We are giving away, losing, never to return, never to benefit. If this is what people mean by altruism, giving without any benefit to the self, then I am not sure it exists, and if it does, I am not sure how good it is either to the individual doing the giving or to the person receiving the gift. Certainly, if I am starving, I would rather receive bread, whether the donor wishes me well or not. But other than in such extreme situations, I do not wish to be served, do not wish to be given to, by someone who is only doing it begrudgingly. And God feels the same: "for God loves a cheerful giver" (2 Corinthians 9:7).

To give without counting the cost is a difficult matter. The prayer of Ignatius of Loyola is well-meaning and has been motivating to many over the years:

> Teach us, good Lord,
> To serve as you deserve,
> To give and not to count the cost,
> To fight and not to heed the wounds,
> To toil and not to seek for rest,
> To labor and not to ask for any reward,
> Save that of knowing that we do your will.

Admirable sentiments indeed, in many ways, and yet I wonder how achievable? Or, when really thought through, how desirable? Should Christians never seek for rest? Should Christians not seek a reward? Is the only reward the knowledge that we are submitting to God's will?

Paul seems to think differently, as he expresses in a most remarkable passage in 2 Corinthians 8–9. There he describes the need for the Corinthian Christians to match or even exceed the generous giving of the Macedonian churches. In these chapters, Paul employs many slightly risky pastoral strategies for stirring up the generosity of the Corinthians, even appropriate competition between the Corinthians and the Macedonians: "See that you excel in this act of grace also" (2 Corinthians 8:7). The Macedonians had received a remarkable grace, evidenced by how they were giving even in the midst of their great difficulties and giving generously, and now

Paul urges the Corinthian Christians to "excel" in this example, to go one better, to beat them.

But apart from such worthy and healthy competitiveness, Paul makes it clear that giving (whether financial or in the whole act of giving of service, here in these chapters referring specifically to the financial) is not a net loss for the generous giver. "The point is this," he writes, "whoever sows sparingly will also reap sparingly, and whoever sows bountifully will also reap bountifully" (2 Corinthians 9:6). The sowing that Paul is referring to here is not the sowing of evangelism or preaching or personal witness, but the sowing of giving financially. As they are generous, Paul predicts, they "will be enriched in every way to be generous in every way, which through us will produce thanksgiving to God" (v. 11).

How does this work? Is Paul saying that God operates like a rather crass Ponzi scheme financial investor? If you give him some money, you are going to get even more back? Certainly not, but on the other hand Paul does say that if the Corinthians give, they won't be lacking for their generosity. "And God is able to make all grace abound to you, so that having all sufficiency in all things at all times, you may abound in every good work" (v. 8). What Paul is saying in these two remarkable chapters on giving is that God is no man's debtor. We are indeed, as Ignatius said, to "give and not count the cost." We are indeed to "serve as you deserve," to "fight [spiritually speaking] and not heed the wounds." Absolutely; give, give, serve, serve, more and more. And yet, this is not to our loss. When we lose ourselves for Christ and his service, we find ourselves.

This does not mean that when we give away our money, we

will receive back even more money, always, without exception, because if that were our motivation, then it would suggest that money was the point, not God. If I give so that I gain money, it means I am not really giving for God. I am investing expecting material, not spiritual, returns. I have made God a sort of "god," a rather small-minded pagan deity who will do what I want if I perform the right rituals or enact the right sacrifices or give the right money (so that I can have more money).

It is true that Jesus does tell us not to "lay up" money but to invest money in heaven, where rust and moth cannot destroy (Matthew 6:20), but this is not saying put your money in a spiritual direction, in a heavenly bank account, because you will have a better return than anywhere else. It is saying to put your heart in heaven and invest in that goal; use even your money as a tool (a powerful tool) for that end. For where your treasure is (heaven), there will be your heart also (Matthew 6:21).

In other words, it really comes down to who Jesus is, who God is, and who we are in relation to him. In some ways, then, the best commentary and explanation of this theme comes in Jesus' sixth of seven "I Am" statements in John's Gospel. This is perhaps the most famous of all of his "I Am" statements, and in some ways the most profound. He is preparing his disciples for his upcoming death and for their role as his emissaries after he has ascended. He is talking to them about the role of the Holy Spirit, the counselor, their commission to represent him, to teach, to be the authoritative spokesmen for him and for the building of his church—these grand themes throughout John 14–16. If anything was a statement of their impending greatness, then these chapters are. In fact, he says, quite explicitly,

> All of giving, all of greatness, all of service, comes down to realizing this one point. Who Jesus is: way, truth, life.

"Truly, truly, I say to you, whoever believes in me will also do the works that I do; and greater works than these will he do, because I am going to the Father" (John 14:12). Jesus is giving them an opportunity to do great things, to be great, to do greater things that even He has done. Not, as many commentators have clarified, meaning that those who follow Jesus will do more impressive miracles than he did—who could do something more impressive than walking on water? But that the greater works they will do will be connected to their mission of pointing people to Jesus. In the New Testament post-Pentecost age, they will be leading people to Christ, filled with the Holy Spirit, and doing this in a far larger way, to a much wider scope, than Jesus had done with his twelve disciples. In this sense they will indeed do, and the church has done, greater works: what greater work could there be than being a part of seeing someone become a New Creation, and seeing that furthered throughout the globe?

So Jesus has something great, greater, for them to do, however exactly we parse what he is saying in that verse. But none of this—not the generosity, not the serving, not the greatness—none of this makes any sense without a clear understanding, belief, and acceptance of who Jesus is, of who God is, and of who we are in relation to him. And then in those famous words of John 14:6, Jesus makes that clear: "Jesus said to him, 'I am the way, and the truth, and the life. No one comes to the Father except through me'" (John 14:6).

What does this famous statement mean? It certainly means that Jesus is the only way to be saved. It certainly means that Jesus is the only way to have a relationship with God the Father. "No one comes to the Father except through me." But it also means that Jesus is truly "the way, and the truth, and the life." He is the way to be saved and the way to the Father, *because* he is the way, the truth, and the life. All of giving, all of greatness, all of service, comes down to realizing this one point. Who Jesus is: way, truth, life.

If this is so, then we do not give asking for no reward save that of knowing that we do God's will; or we do that, but knowing there is far more. We give, knowing that we are giving to the One who is the way, truth, and life. We serve, knowing that we are serving the One who is the way, truth, and life. We don't want to just know that we are *doing* his will; we want to know that we are *in* his will, that we are following his way, that we are connected to his life, that we have his truth. If all of life, all of truth, all of the way, the path, the existence, the everything is Jesus, then to give all to Jesus is not losing, it is gaining. It must be so by definition.

Let me use an illustration. Say you are playing a game of basketball and, for some reason, you have the opportunity to give your basketball away, so that it goes through the hoop at the opposition's end of the court and gets you a basket. Have you lost? Are you still holding the basketball? No, you gave it away, but you gave it away for the purpose of the game.

Same with Jesus. When we give him money, when we serve

him, when we worship him, we begin to realize true greatness. It is not that he needs the money or needs us to serve him in order to get things done or desperately requires another contemporary worship song or old hymn; it is that he is the way, the truth, and the life. And to give to him, to serve him, is not to lose; it is (in a somewhat crass metaphor) to score a basket. This is what the game of life is about.

EXPAND

As such, expansion, effort, improvement, goal setting, and achievement are not bad for this purpose, and for this person; they are good; they are all good—for he is the way, the truth, and the life. We should positively delight in this kind of greatness, being servant of all, for him who is the all in all.

The sixth of the seven letters of Jesus to the churches in Asia in Revelation emphasizes this kind of greatness and shows us how at the root of it is faithfulness to God, to Jesus, and to his word. It is this principle that will cause us to be excellent, great, in the truest and most biblical sense.

> And to the angel of the church in Philadelphia write: "The words of the holy one, the true one, who has the key of David, who opens and no one will shut, who shuts and no one opens. I know your works. Behold, I have set before you an open door, which no one is able to shut. I know that you have but little power, and yet you have kept my word and have not denied my name. Behold, I will make those of the synagogue of Satan who say that they are Jews and are not, but

lie—behold, I will make them come and bow down before your feet, and they will learn that I have loved you. Because you have kept my word about patient endurance, I will keep you from the hour of trial that is coming on the whole world, to try those who dwell on the earth. I am coming soon. Hold fast what you have, so that no one may seize your crown. The one who conquers, I will make him a pillar in the temple of my God. Never shall he go out of it, and I will write on him the name of my God, and the name of the city of my God, the new Jerusalem, which comes down from my God out of heaven, and my own new name. He who has an ear, let him hear what the Spirit says to the churches." (Revelation 3:7-13)

We tend to think of achievement and greatness along "pragmatic" lines; that is, we tend to think that achievement is based upon what works. Today pragmatism rules the roost. Pragmatism is the doctrine, long-since established, that the way to succeed is to do what works. This seems so obvious nowadays that the very statement of the opinion almost appears tautologous. Originally a philosophic school stating that the test of truth is its practical results, these days pragmatism is the underlying assumption of much of our lives. And nowhere more so than in the realm of religion—we want to know that this God-character is going to have some good results; we want Christianity to be practical. And this is all reasonable enough, inevitable enough, it appears to us.

But actually pragmatism is more than this and has more insidious effects than this. It is not just the belief in such truisms of everyday life, such as "If it ain't broke, don't fix it."

It is not just being "practical" and "down-to-earth." Pragmatism has a tendency to downgrade all endeavors after truth or beauty to the lowest common denominator. If it is not quantifiable, pragmatism tends to end up suggesting it is not true, or at least not worthy of being considered for long. It is pure pragmatism to question the validity of art galleries. After all, are they really producing any practical results? And it is pure pragmatism to defend the validity of art galleries solely on the basis of how many people attended last year. Such statistics are quantifiable, practical, pragmatic in its pure sense. It is pure pragmatism to question the value of intellectual achievements in their purest sense. Universities and professors then become training programs for producing a more effective economy—and if classes and schools cannot match this criterion, then they are appropriately questioned by this all-pervasive pragmatic spirit.

The trouble with such things is that while obviously, and clearly, having good results is a test of truth, it is not the *only* test of truth or worth, and what's more, it can be an elusive test of truth and value. For instance, the good results of teaching someone about higher mathematics or the beauty of a painting are not readily quantifiable. They are, nonetheless, there. Some of the greatest—and let it be said, practical—technological advances of recent years came about as a result of research into pure theoretical mathematics, research that was funded not for a pragmatic reason but out of a principled commitment to the advance of human knowledge.

In other words, one cannot always tell what is going to have the best result. And if the best, most practical result is the *only* and the *dominant* guiding criterion, then much that will actually produce good results if left to its own will fall by the wayside. What room is there for beauty, truth, love, the higher virtues, in a purely pragmatic universe? Unmitigated pragmatism is the strip mall of truth.

It is interesting to note, then, that the church of Philadelphia, one of only two churches in these seven letters of Revelation to receive praise without criticism from the lips of the Lord Jesus, is a church that, pragmatically speaking, has "little power." Yet it is commended as the model of a healthy church. Unlike Smyrna, the other church that receives pure praise from Jesus, it is excellent not only in its current faithfulness but also for its future usefulness. It is, in fact, a church with enormous pragmatic opportunities—it has "an open door."

> If we have a low view of Scripture, soon enough we will have a low view of Christ.

And yet none of this comes from a pragmatic approach but rather from a principled commitment to keeping Jesus' word. It is this that they have "held on to" or "kept," which is emphasized in verse 10: "you have kept my word about patient endurance." It is this word of Jesus, the word of God, that is the controlling principle of greatness that defines the Philadelphian church.

So the sixth letter to the churches of Revelation is teaching us that greatness is being word-driven: focused, compelled, attracted, and motivated by God's word. It brings attention to the word of God as the principle of greatness in three ways. First, it tells us, "This is what honors Jesus." Second, it tells us that this is what "creates opportunities." Third, it tells us that this principle "is actually what truly works."

Greatness Is Word-Driven, for This Is "What Honors Jesus"

Keeping God's word is always connected here to what honors Jesus. In verse 8, keeping the word is connected to having not denied Jesus' name. The name of Jesus is his character, his reputation, his honor. "You have kept my word and have not denied my name." Because they have done this, Jesus himself, so honored, will bring others to acknowledge that he has loved them. Verse 9: "I will make them come and bow down before your feet, and they will learn that I have loved you." Since, verse 10, they have kept his word about patient endurance, he will also keep them from "the hour of trial." And then, in verse 12, so faithful to Jesus are they that it is on them that Jesus will write his name, the name of the city of God, and the name of God. The word is what exalts the Lord Jesus: his name and his love are connected to the church that holds on to the word.

We think of the word of God as something intellectual. For Jesus, it is personal. It is *his* word. It is, in fact, the word of his "patient endurance." That phrase may indicate a specific command in Scripture to endure patiently. Much more likely, in my view, it indicates the personal suffering that the message of Christ involves. It is his word about patient endurance, or of his suffering: it is the word of Christ, the suffering servant.

They have held on to that, and not rejected the cross of Jesus that the word of Jesus speaks about. Those who reject the word soon enough downplay the cross and before long deny the name. It is the word of Jesus that witnesses to the exclusive Lordship of Jesus—his being the *only* way of being saved, his cross, his sufferings, his patient endurance, winning for us who believe salvation from death and hell, this word witnesses to the name. And if we have a low view of Scripture, soon enough we will have a low view of Christ. But if we hold on to the word, we honor Jesus. It is his word. He gave his blood for it. It is personal, not just intellectual. The word honors Jesus. It exalts him. It shows his love and his name.

But Bible study is so boring. It is so dry. What we need is technological pyrotechnics—that will bring the people in! What we need is more entertainment! Why do we need to explain the Bible? We all know what it says anyway. We need surveys; we need results. The last thing in the world we need is the Bible; let's keep it on the shelf; let's have it on the podium. Let's have brief motivational messages about life, which occasionally refer to a bit in the Bible, and then we can excite everyone and sort of associate God with the excitement. That'll work.

Well, actually, it won't work, as we'll see. But neither will it honor Jesus. It cost him his life, this word. Keeping to it may cost us something. In Franklin Graham's book *The Name*, he describes how he was pilloried for praying in the name of the Lord Jesus at the inauguration of the president of the United States. There is something deeply offensive in the exclusive claims to worship of the Lord Jesus Christ. Sticking to what the Bible says about Jesus may cost us patient endurance too, a cross too, as it cost Jesus the cross. But if we honor Jesus, if we love Jesus, we will keep the word at the heart of our churches. It is a defining test of our relationship to Jesus. You can't say you respect me and twist my word for your ends. Neither can you say you honor Jesus and not let his word set the direction of your life.

GREATNESS IS WORD-DRIVEN BECAUSE "IT CREATES OPPORTUNITIES"

The "open door" has been given various interpretations by scholars (Revelation 3:7-8). Some have said it is an open door of prayer. Others have said it is an open door of missionary expansion. Others still have said it is an open door of access to God through Christ, an open door of salvation. Others again have thought that it is an open door of entrance to the kingdom when Jesus returns. I think it is all of these.

Let me explain. The phrase "open door" has various possible uses. A little later in this chapter, it means being willing to repent: "Behold, I stand at the door and knock. If anyone hears my voice and opens the door, I will come in to him and eat with him, and he with me" (Revelation 3:20). At the beginning of chapter 4, it means the extraordinary access that John was given to the throne room of heaven: "After this I looked, and behold, a door standing open in heaven!" The apostle Paul characteristically used the phrase of missionary opportunities. He asked the Colossian church to pray that a door would be opened for his ministry; he gave thanks for an open door to the

Corinthian church. This is how the phrase is used in the Acts of the Apostles as well.

The point here in Philadelphia is that the messianic fruition was in the hands of the church and no other religious institution. In verse 3:7, Christ holds the "key of David," a reference to Isaiah 22:22. He can open the door. He has opened the door for the church. And in verse 9, those who think they have understood the message of the Old Testament, who claim to be the inheritors of the promise of Abraham but have not combined that with faith in Jesus and his word, will come to realize the genuineness of the Christian church and worship with them the Lord Jesus: "I will make them come and bow down before your feet, and they will learn that I have loved you." Incidentally, if you're ever tempted to think that the Bible is anti-Semitic, you just need to remember that the people writing this were ethnically Jews (Jesus was a Jew). The point is not ethnic; it is religious. Who has real access to God? Who has the power of the keys of the kingdom? Who is engaging in true worship of God? It is the Christian church through the gift of Jesus.

So the "open door" here could mean anything that characterizes those on the inside track with God. It could mean freedom in prayer, it could mean access to God, it could mean salvation, but most particularly it is explained here in verse 9 to mean evangelistic success. They will "bow down"; that is the word used for "worship"; they will become worshipers of Jesus too, join and together enjoy the fruit of the messianic kingdom of the Lord Jesus, who has the key of David, and through whom heaven itself is an open door.

Greatness Is Word-Driven Because "It Works"

> Because you have kept my word about patient endur-
> ance, I will keep you from the hour of trial that is com-
> ing on the whole world, to try those who dwell on the
> earth. I am coming soon. Hold fast what you have,
> so that no one may seize your crown. The one who
> conquers, I will make him a pillar in the temple of my
> God. Never shall he go out of it, and I will write on
> him the name of my God, and the name of the city of
> my God, the new Jerusalem, which comes down from
> my God out of heaven, and my own new name. (Rev-
> elation 3:10-12)

These verses initially appear near impenetrable but are well
illustrated by an insight into the scene of Philadelphia itself.

Like Sardis, Philadelphia had been devastated in the catastrophic earthquake of AD 17. Sardis was initially more seri-
ously affected, but Philadelphia, being nearer to the epicenter
of the quake, suffered aftershocks, it seems, for a long time
thereafter. In fact, the residents of the city took to living outside of the city in the open plain to avoid the danger of the
unpredictable, constantly falling debris. Philadelphia was a city
famous for its religious and athletic festivals, so much that it
was called "little Athens." It was also well known for its wine.
Right on the edge of the volcanic material of the area, and volcanic rock being good for growing vines, it established wealth
through its wine trade. It was also a gateway city. It had two

important trade routes running through it, and had initially probably been established as a missionary city of Greek culture and language.

All these diverse local conditions are important for understanding what's going on here, for the emperor enacted a disastrous command in AD 92 whereby about half of the local vines were destroyed. It may have been to encourage the growing of wheat instead, but this government action came near to destroying the economy of Philadelphia because, although being an ideal region for growing vines, it was probably less ideal for growing wheat.

The "hour of trial" in verse 10 speaks to the suffering. It is a peculiar expression. Only here and in Hebrews 3:8 in the New Testament is the article *the* used before the word *trial* (*testing* in Hebrews). Literally, it is "the hour of the trial." It indicates something specific. And something that went over the whole of the world. Again, the phrase was used to indicate the inhabited earth as distinct from the non-Roman world. It was an issue for the empire. It is quite possible then that this hour of trial is *the* hour of *the* trial that was unwittingly released on the Roman world. It was particularly barbaric because no one, not even conquering armies, destroyed vines or olive trees because they took so long to grow to maturity and their destruction could mean the starvation of the people.

The "crown" is the well-known athletic wreath given to the victor in athletic conquests, especially appropriate for "little Athens." The promise "Never shall he go out of it" was especially heartwarming for a people who had to flee an earthquake-devastated city time and time again.

In other words, what Jesus is saying is that this spiritual, principled commitment to the word works in practice. They have held on to the word; he is going to hold on to them, come hell or high water—or judgment or famine.

It works in the present, as seen in verse 10. During the famine they will be held on to and protected. Not taken out of the situation—as Jesus prayed for his disciples that God would not take them out of the world but that they would be protected from the evil one—not taken out of the situation but kept from the specific hour of trial about to arrive.

It works for the future too, as in verses 11 and 12: "I am coming soon." In the word *soon*, Jesus speaks in the sense of imminently, not speedily. This is referring to Jesus' second coming. Hold on to what they have (What are they holding on to? The word!) so that they do not lose their crown of victory in this testing conquest for their souls. And he who does hold on to the word and "overcome" will be made a pillar—that is, secure, stable, and not shaken.

Excellence and greatness is to hold on to the word.

And never again will he leave it. He will have the name of God, of the city of God, and of Jesus himself invested in him. That is, those who have kept Jesus' word and therefore honored Jesus' name will be privileged to have that name, that honor, that commitment relayed to them for eternity in the city of God. The writing of the name is an Old Testament image picked up in various ways indicating ownership. Just as we write our names on something to say it is ours, so Jesus is saying that because of our commitment to him and his word and his name, he is committed to us now and for all eternity.

It is a wonderful passage. The excellent or great church holds on to the word, for this honors Jesus, it creates opportunities, and it works even in the very practicalities of economic challenge and eternal destiny.

Strangely enough, however, in a few years after this was written, the excellent church of Philadelphia was struggling. Ignatius, passing through on his way to martyrdom in Rome, noted a Judaizing divisive tendency to despise the New Testament word, the apostolic word and the word of Jesus that had been their great achievement. And a little later still, a sect called the Montanists rose up to shake the Christian world with their claim to a new word, a prophetic inspiration, which led to the denial of the word of Jesus. Surprisingly, it seems pretty clear that Philadelphia was the birthplace of these Montanists.

How could this be? We can see the seeds of the trouble even here. The Montanists claimed that the promise of the coming kingdom of the Lord Jesus would be fulfilled right now on earth and claimed that the city of God had descended from heaven. The Judaizers sought God speaking primarily in the Old Testament, the Jewish Scriptures. Both forgot to hold on to the word, which is why verse 11 is so appropriate. "Hold fast to what you have." Do not give way to a supercharged spirituality that claims to overwrite the once-and-for-all faith delivered to the saints. Do not give way to a legalistic moralism that denies the saving word of Jesus in favor of the law. Instead, excellence and greatness is to hold on to the word.

Even if his word is to give away your money and follow him.

A Day for Glory

*Jesus said to them "Truly, I say to you, in the new world,
when the Son of Man will sit on his glorious throne, you
who have followed me will also sit on twelve thrones,
judging the twelve tribes of Israel."*

—Matthew 19:28

This Sunday, instead of the movie *Four Weddings and a Funeral*, I offer you two funerals and a wedding.

The first funeral was for a former drug dealer. She had been on the streets of New York and elsewhere, living a life about which the less said the better. She had done things about which she was not proud and had been involved with activities—on a consistent basis—that were not only highly illegal but also downright shoddy. Her life had spun on its way for a decade or two in this fashion, until, in the middle of her life, she hit rock bottom. She came to the end of herself, and still a well-known drug dealer in the area, she nonetheless found herself with no money to speak of and living in a homeless shelter.

It was there that Christ found her. Gradually she was won to the gospel, was converted, was baptized, and became a member of a local church. She started to try to reach out to her friends, family, and former connections. Then she became sick. She was diagnosed with liver failure, the fruit of her previous lifestyle, and slowly she started to slip away from this life.

When she had finally died, arrangements were made for her funeral and her burial so that she would be buried near the place where she had dealt drugs before she had become a Christian. It was some sort of testimony, I suppose. At the funeral, a strange thing occurred. Her daughter, who had not yet come to know the Lord, got up from her seat and sat down in the front of the church next to the coffin. She wept uncontrollably. Eventually a relative came to comfort her and try to lead her back to her place.

As the service finished and the coffin was carried out to the waiting hearse, the family and friends departed the building. And then when the coffin was put into the back of the hearse, the daughter actually climbed into the back of the car as well, and clung to the coffin inside the vehicle. She was beside herself and could not be comforted at that time. Her mother had died: who could blame her?

The other funeral was very different. It was the funeral of a young man, an upstanding Christian man. In the first funeral I described, the mother had become a Christian, but the daughter had not yet put the pieces together of an eternal hope. In this second funeral, however, all of the family seemed clearly to be Christians, as far as anyone can ever tell. The feeling of the funeral was quite different.

Yet the circumstances were no less tragic, perhaps more so. This young man came from a missionary family to an inner-city urban area. His father had died of cancer, and now, at a very young age, this young man also had suddenly developed a fast-working tumor that ate away at his body, and in apparently no time at all left him dead. The family was well-known and much loved in the community, and the church was packed wall to wall with well-wishers, friends, and family members. The young man in whose short life so much had been achieved was commended, but all the time Jesus was exalted through every part of the commendation and every part of the service.

At the end, when the coffin came to be moved to the back of the church and out to the waiting hearse, there was a very different conclusion to that which took place in the first funeral I described. This time, as the mother walked behind the coffin—a woman who had buried her husband from cancer and was now burying her son as a young man—there was no despair. She mourned, of course, but with each step that the funeral procession took down the aisle, the mother could be heard saying over and over again, "Praise you, Jesus. Praise you, Jesus."

Funerals bring into clear focus many things we believe about life, and much that we hope for (or fear) about the life to come. If we have no hope for a future beyond the grave, then the best a funeral can offer us is the chance to say good-bye, and depending upon our personality or our ability to be stoic, that good-bye can appear more or less traumatic to those watching. Sometimes, of course, those who are aware that they will soon be leaving us can give us messages of comfort that can attempt to sugar the bitter pill of being forced to say good-bye to them—even messages of reassurance. A loved one may tell us that we are not to worry about them because they feel that they have had a full life and have not missed out on anything. This sort of reassurance can offer us comfort at the time of departing, and it can offer us comfort as we face our own departure, but it cannot offer us hope beyond the grave.

Because of that we tend today to try to create a "good death," even wanting to determine the time of our own passing rather than letting "nature take its course" and to die (understandably enough) with minimum pain. Often our last moments are so controlled that we are not aware of much, as our responses are dimmed so that our pain is not felt. The downside of these medical miracles is that we are not able to prepare for the great journey through the veil to the other side in the way that previous generations did. Augustine, we are told, even spent a whole week before his death, doing nothing other than readying his heart and his soul to meet his Maker.

Augustine, usually thought to be one of the greatest Christian leaders of his and any age, was a highly moral man who followed Jesus with great strictness and integrity. Yet as it became clear that his passing was near, he asked all those attending on him to give him the space to make his confessions and prepare his heart for this final step. He asked not to be disturbed beyond necessity, beyond meal times, and the rest of what was to be his final week in this world was given over to prayer, contemplation, and preparation for the coming death and the encounter with his Maker.

These days, much of that week typically might be spent in a

morphine haze. Having been at many a sickbed and a deathbed or two, I can attest to the marvel of modern abilities to control pain and am certainly grateful for it. There are times when such extreme pain management medication is a wonderful—blessed even—relief.

But our attitudes toward death and the life to come have become void of much reality. We tend to dismiss the topic quickly, as if we could avoid our own death by not talking about it too much. Perhaps we do not feel we have much in the way of answers, so we prefer not to raise the uncomfortable questions.

Previous generations of Christians had a very different attitude toward death and developed a distinctive culture about it. The Puritans had a whole literature of deathbed statements to prepare minds for mortality, and even the ancient pagans seemed ready to face up to the realities of the grave. The great Roman poet Horace said that "pale death kicks his way equally into the cottages of the poor and the castles of kings." But you would not find much popular music or literature about the subject of dying today. The one rather surprising exception to this general rule of silence about death—the modern taboo—is the last book in the Harry Potter series, which in addition to many other things, deals consistently with the matter of death, the question about what is to come after death, and how to avoid death.

The reason for this understandable desire not to face up to the reality of our own mortality on any regular basis is simple enough: fear. The First Duke of Wellington is said to have remarked, "A person must be a coward or a liar who can boast of never having felt a fear of death." And that from a British

There is a remedy for death.

general who probably saw more than his fair share of death, no doubt, and risked his own life more than most. But the result of not dealing with life's great question, and not living this life in the light of the answer to that great question, is so much of our lives are petty, meaningless, and puerile. We live as children amassing toys, toys that we cannot take with us, like children playing video games on a plane that's about to crash. We entertain ourselves and develop hobbies and pastimes as if this life, with its great shortness of breath, were not a too-precious material, in very limited short supply, of which we simply cannot afford to let the time pass.

American correspondent, Robert D. Abrahams, said:

> Most men die inch by inch
> Playing little games.[1]

It's easy for all of us to feel that we are spending our lives "playing little games." Maneuvering for position, perhaps; climbing the corporate ladder, perhaps; even worthy endeavors, like bringing up our children, can seem a bit pointless at times, when the little tyke behaves badly, or the teenager rebels, or the adult child forgets that you exist. We seem, often enough, to be on a journey of dying inch by inch, and all because—it seems—we live under the shadow of the biggest fear of them all. As Don Quixote said, "There is a remedy for everything except death."

But there is a remedy for death. It is simply but wonderfully expressed in the poem "Conversion" by Frances Angermayer, written in 1943:

> Well, I'll have to go now, God—Goodbye.
> Strange since I met you, I'm not afraid to die.[2]

A big part of following Jesus is coming to the point where we are no longer afraid to die, however much we still might not relish the prospect of the actual process of death. This is something that Jesus promised to "you who have followed me"; not the emotional absence of fear, but the removal of any doubt as to our eternal destiny. Those who have followed him will also "sit on twelve thrones"; we will be in an elevated place, "with him in glory," in the age to come, the new heaven and the new earth, "in which righteousness dwells" (as Peter put it in 2 Peter 3:13), a "crown," not only for such greats as the apostle Paul but also for "all who have loved his appearing" (2 Timothy 4:8).

CHURCH

I said that there were going to be two funerals and a wedding. The wedding comes now and is connected to the church. It was on "the Lord's Day" (our Sunday) that John saw the vision that he recorded in the Book of Revelation, and his vision centers on Christ and his church. So we find in Revelation 21 that he begins now to describe a wedding, the wedding between "the Bride" (the church) and Christ, the groom.

"Come," the angel says to John and John records for us.

"Come, I will show you the Bride, the wife of the Lamb. And he carried me away in the Spirit to a great, high mountain, and showed me the holy city Jerusalem coming down out of heaven from God, having the glory of God, its radiance like a most rare jewel, like a jasper, clear as crystal" (Revelation 21:9-11).

For many of us heaven feels like a purely individual experience, but biblically heaven is something experienced not only individually but also by God's people together, his church. This "Bride," this "wife of the Lamb," this "holy city Jerusalem" has the "glory of God." Our human marriages and weddings are testimonies, pointers, and descriptors of this ultimate, primordial, and predicted wedding. So the apostle Paul in Ephesians 5 describes how Christians are to behave in marriage, and then concludes this instruction to say that all of this is really referring to "Christ and the church." In other words, our marriages point to this greater marriage still to come, "heaven," the "glory of God." This is a "mystery" Paul says, that is, a thing that was hidden, which is now revealed, connected profoundly to the preaching of the gospel, the mystery of Christ's love for the church (Ephesians 5:32 and surrounding), consummated finally in this "glory of God," which John describes.

This is a wedding to beat any wedding! With every human wedding, however godly and beautiful the couple, there is a mixture of hope and apprehension. We hope that all will turn out right, but we also know that suffering will come; there will be battles to fight and obstacles to overcome. Marriage is hard work because it is the joining together of two sinners, two people fallen, as well as two people made in the image of God.

But what would it be like if marriage were not like that?

What if it were the joining together of two people without a flaw, without a selfish bone in their bodies and without any suffering or tears to come? Ah, that would be heaven.

And so it would, yet more so. Marriage is designed to whisper in our pain of a greater joy to come, in which all of God's people can participate. When something so potentially beautiful and perfect is also so wrought with disappointment, it can mean only one of two things. It could mean that the original potential was misleading, that the seller of marriage hawked us something not true, not real, a lie. Or it could mean that the potential of marriage is fulfilled on a farther horizon. The Bible says it is the latter: marriage tells us that there is something more to come, and it tells us this not only in its wonderful joys even now but also in every moment that disappoints. It says to us, "Surely there is more to life than this." And the answer is that there is.

Without that, we have some sympathy with the statement made by Vladimir Nabokov, the author of the very controversial novel *Lolita*, in the first sentence of his autobiography: "The cradle rocks above an abyss, and common sense tells us that existence is but a brief crack of light between two eternities of darkness."[3] When we begin to look at the Christian hope of glory against the backdrop of this common view of the darkness around which life is surrounded, we can see that the resurrection of Jesus is much more than simply a "proof" that there is life to come after death. The ancient world commonly held that life in some shape or form continued after death, but what the resurrection of Jesus proclaimed was the resurrection of the body. That there would not be, in glory, simply a place for the soul but also a place for the body, a resurrected, changed, immortal body, to be sure, but still the body. And it is this hope that shines light into the darkness, that tells us that the cradle is not simply rocking above the grave, but that marriage, family, birth, life itself, is a mystery that beckons to be unraveled in the mystery of the gospel, centered on the death and resurrection of Jesus Christ himself.

ETERNITY

The last of Jesus' seven signs in John's Gospel points very clearly to this resurrection being the ultimate context of God's glory. Jesus himself, God himself, is the center of glory; this glory is revealed in Christ; this glory is displayed for us, in which we share, in the new heaven and the new earth to come, in the Resurrection. And so in the last of these seven signs, Jesus comes to the tomb of Lazarus, dead now so long that there would be a stench from his rotting remains. "Lord, by this time there will be an odor, for he has been dead four days," Martha says. Jesus replied to this very human, practical, and real concern with a question, "Did I not tell you that if you believed you would see the glory of God?" This glory that they will "see" is going to be shown in the raising of Lazarus from the dead. And so with a "loud voice," Jesus cries out, having prayed publicly so that others can listen in and realize that

> "Death is swallowed up in victory."
> "O death, where is your victory?
> O death, where is your sting?"

Jesus has been sent by God: "'Lazarus, come out.' The man who had died came out, his hands and feet bound with linen strips and his face wrapped with a cloth. Jesus said to them, 'Unbind him, and let him go'" (John 11:39-44).

This glory, the glory of Lazarus being raised from the dead, is not the permanent, ultimate glory, for Lazarus will himself die before he is raised again. But it is a sign, a thing pointing beyond itself, a miracle to say something, show something, about the resurrection to come. It is the last of the seven signs in John's Gospel, which "are written so that you may believe that Jesus is the Christ, the Son of God, and that by believing you may have life in his name" (John 20:31). Lazarus's raising, in particular, seems to have caused many people at the time to put their faith in Jesus, which makes it somewhat surprising that the other Gospels do not emphasize this particular miracle to which John gives so much space. Perhaps the other Gospel writers simply emphasize other themes in their eyewitness accounts.

In any case, the raising of Lazarus is a "glory." It tells us of that day when, rotting and decomposing in our tomb, we will hear a voice crying out our names, saying, "Come out!" Many Christians believe in what is called the "intermediate state"; that is, when we are away from the body, we are at home with the Lord (2 Corinthians 5:8), to be with him in glory, and yet there is still also a resurrection to come when

> the dead will be raised imperishable, and we shall be changed. For this perishable body must put on the imperishable, and this mortal body must put on immortality. When the perishable puts on the

imperishable, and the mortal puts on immortality, then shall come to pass the saying that is written:

> "Death is swallowed up in victory."
> "O death, where is your victory?
> O death, where is your sting?"

The sting of death is sin, and the power of sin is the law. But thanks be to God, who gives us the victory through our Lord Jesus Christ. (1 Corinthians 15:52-57)

This world, this life, this "age," "will be set on fire and dissolved, and the heavenly bodies will melt as they burn!" This whole present reality will pass away. Those who die in the Lord before that great and awful day will go to be at home with Jesus, "at home with the Lord," personally and immediately upon death. And then, on that final day, "according to his promise we are waiting for new heavens and a new earth in which righteousness dwells" (2 Peter 3:12-13). This is the "day of the Lord," and for those who have repented (*metanoia*) and believed in (*mysterion*) the gospel, this day will be a day of glory.

Such a terrible, fearful prospect inevitably—and rightly—raises a greater fear than the mere fear of death. There will be not just glory but judgment. That judgment will be based on the holiness and righteousness of God, and the new heaven and new earth will be the home of righteousness. Those who are not righteous will be cast into outer darkness, where there is weeping and gnashing of teeth, where the fire is not quenched and the worm does not die. No more terrible and fearful a day could there possibly be. And the great question, which the New Testament and the whole of the Bible seek to answer, is: how can I be sure that I am an inheritor of glory and not damnation?

There are certainly many good works that we are called to do as Christians. We are called to feed the poor, to visit those in prison, to clothe the destitute, to care for one another, so that there are no poor among us in fulfillment of the Old Testament promise that the New Testament people are the people of God always designed by God to be. We are to not give up meeting together; we are to worship in spirit and in truth; we are to be perfect as our heavenly Father is perfect. Our righteousness is to surpass that of the Pharisees. In short, the standards, the requirements, are quite unachievable, and easily acknowledged to be unachievable, to all but the gross hypocrite or the unconsciously self-deceived or intolerably self-righteous.

Who is equal to these things? Answer: no one. There is no one righteous, not even one. We are all sinners alike, and to quote the Anglican prayer book, "There is no health in us." But God is the same Lord whose nature is always to have mercy. These requirements, written in stone and confirmed in the law of Christ in the New Testament, are the fruit of God's work in us. They are not the root. They are not the cause of God's work in us, and they are not what saves us, but they are what show that we have been saved. Our judgment is based upon the righteousness of Christ, for if it is based upon our own righteousness, then "be perfect, as your heavenly Father is perfect." And that is a standard that none can reach.

So, in the last of the seven "I Am" statements of Jesus in

John's Gospel, we come across his well-known statement that "I am the true vine" (John 15:1).

The vine is a metaphor drawn from the Old Testament of God's people. The vine is God's people in covenant with God, and God (the Father) is the vinedresser. Now Jesus says that he is the vine. He is the perfect Son that Israel—and all of God's people—never was and never could be. "No one is righteous." He is the "true vine." And what that means is that we can be a part of that by being "in" that vine. We are not the vine itself; we are the branches. And Christ calls us to "abide," or remain, in him. "I am the vine; you are the branches. Whoever abides in me and I in him, he it is that bears much fruit, for apart from me you can do nothing" (John 15:5). *Apart from me you can do nothing.* It is only as we "abide" in him that we bear much fruit. He is the vine, the source of righteousness, power, ability, joy, connection to the father; as the "sap" flows from him to us, the branches, *then* we "bear much fruit."

When a person, in full awareness of all of his sins—not needing nor wanting to pretend—faces his destiny and hears the death rattle coming toward him, his confidence in the future is not based upon "being perfect as the heavenly Father is perfect." His confidence is in "abiding" in Jesus, remaining in him: he who died for sinners and whose life was given for theirs that they can bear much fruit, fruit even unto glory.

CHURCH AND ETERNITY

With such confidence our lives now are very different. But the end goal of such a vision of glory is not to make our lives now different, though that is one of its "fruits." The point is that it leads us to glory itself. A vision of glory is not utilitarian, any more than a vision of God is simply to make us better or happier. The goal is God; the goal is glory; Jesus is the vine; we are the branches. Yet as we "abide" in him by faith, trusting, then we find a new vision, and hope overflows.

Trust is a much-misunderstood word, only beaten for this award by its even more abused older cousin *faith*. We tend to think of faith as passive, as intellectual, as cognitive, and our tendency in that regard is not much helped by people telling us that "faith is a verb" because if faith is a "doing" word, but we're not sure what it is we're meant to be doing—for whom or why or how—then faith is different from works. Trust, likewise, tends to give us the impression of trustworthiness, and at worst gullibility, because we certainly know not everyone is trustworthy. Frederick Buechner tells the story of when one day he was in a quandary over the illness of his daughter, a car drove by bearing the single word "trust." For him it was not just a chance event, but a moment of revelation, if you like, of insight, of God speaking, of the need simply to trust. With such trust we are connected to God, to each other, and to eternity.

Trust is ultimately a humble thing. The man or woman who has everything has no need to rely upon anyone else, and trust at its heart means the opposite of self-reliance.

In our last of the seven letters of Christ to the churches in Revelation, we come across a church that felt it was doing just fine and needed to learn what it meant to rely upon Jesus.

And to the angel of the church in Laodicea write: "The words of the Amen, the faithful and true witness, the beginning of God's creation. I know your works: you are neither cold nor hot. Would that you were either cold or hot! So, because you are lukewarm, and neither hot nor cold, I will spit you out of my mouth. For you say, I am rich, I have prospered, and I need nothing, not realizing that you are wretched, pitiable, poor, blind, and naked. I counsel you to buy from me gold refined by fire, so that you may be rich, and white garments so that you may clothe yourself and the shame of your nakedness may not be seen, and salve to anoint your eyes, so that you may see. Those whom I love, I reprove and discipline, so be zealous and repent. Behold, I stand at the door and knock. If anyone hears my voice and opens the door, I will come in to him and eat with him, and he with me. The one who conquers, I will grant him to sit with me on my throne, as I also conquered and sat down with my Father on his throne. He who has an ear, let him hear what the Spirit says to the churches." (Revelation 3:14-22)

At a human level, the opposite of self-reliance is friendship, and friendship has indeed long been viewed as a great delight. The ancients thought friendship one of the most precious of all human experiences. The Victorians waxed lyrical on the subject. Modern life, however, may have created a situation where genuine friendship is becoming comparatively rare. Evidence of this is not hard to find. Men, in particular, seem these days to find it challenging to have real, deep friends.

We could suggest various explanations for why this is so. It could have something to do with modern Western life. Outside the West, friendship is showing no sign of abating, while in the West the predom-

Jesus is necessary even for the wealthy, even for the beautiful, and even for the healthy.

inance of counselors and self-help books can function as surrogate friends, in at least some, if by no means all, instances. In fast-paced American society who, after all, has *time* for friendship? Or the emotional energy required? And how many people are there left who spend enough of their lives in one town to build real, deep friends?

We still want profound friendship, but it is an ideal that recedes over the horizon of possibility with each new demand made upon us, each new geographical relocation, each new wound we pick up from an attempted quick-fix relationship.

Other, more pressing matters take up our attention. Like economic survival. Like family. Like study. Like work. Like getting through the 5 to 7 p.m. daily crisis hour of family life.

All of which, a Laodicean might say, makes it good to know that when we come to the subject of religion, we can gladly leave our emotional vulnerability behind. We don't really need to engage with God personally, at a deep friendship level; we merely need to go through the motions, to enact the ritual. In fact, of course, the church itself is an institution that has as its ideal the establishment of such a stable edifice that the vulnerability of spiritual engagement is no longer necessary. We don't need to cry out to God for funds; we have the money in an investment fund in the bank. It doesn't matter if we lose a person or two from church; after all, there are still plenty more. And God himself can be helpfully kept at arm's distance, outside the parameter of our emotional and vulnerable center, necessary yet not engaged.

Jean-Henri Merle d'Aubigné, one of the preeminent historians of the Reformation, summarized that it was exactly this haughtiness of self-reliance that led that movement, which began so well, to become embroiled in worldly politics.[4] And it was exactly this issue facing the church in Laodicea.

We have seen in these seven letters to the seven churches of Asia the different needs of the churches and the Lord Jesus' remedy for each. To the Ephesians, who had lost their first love, Christ calls them back to remember. To Smyrna, facing martyrdom, Christ calls them to bravery. To Pergamum, corrupted by doctrinal compromise, Christ calls them to disciplined consistency. To Thyatira, sullied by moral compromise, Christ calls them to purity. To Sardis, sleepy Sardis, Christ calls "Awake," to put their trust not in their incomplete deeds but in him. To Philadelphia, commended, he urges them to continue to hold on to the word. Now, finally in Laodicea, we have a church that needs nothing!

"You say, I am rich, I have prospered, and I need nothing" (Revelation 3:17). They were fine. It was sweet of Jesus to have written them a personal letter, but they had a perfectly good organization. They didn't need money! They didn't need him! But what Jesus is saying here is that he is necessary even for the wealthy, even for the beautiful, and even for the healthy.

JESUS IS NECESSARY EVEN FOR THE WEALTHY

"I know your works; you are neither cold nor hot.
Would that you were either cold or hot! So, because
you are lukewarm, and neither hot nor cold, I will spit
you out of my mouth." (Revelation 3:15-16)

But they think they're wealthy so they need nothing, when,
in fact, they are not, and in verse 18, Jesus suggests they need
to buy "gold refined by fire" from him. Put these together and
we get the picture of what was going on in Laodicea.

Laodicea was a remarkably rich city. It was a banking center, in which even famous Cicero cashed his checks. Its wealth
was based on a number of different factors. One of these was
its location. It was at the crossroads of several important trading routes. Sir William Ramsay, great archaeologist and New
Testament scholar, thought of it as a "knot" of a road system.[5]
Here the city had every opportunity for advancing in financial wealth by trading. So attractive was its wealth that there
are records of rabbis complaining at the Jewish Diaspora being
drawn to Laodicea for its baths, gymnasiums, and general good
time.

Despite this, however, it had one great vulnerability: its
water supply. Its location had been chosen for the road system, not for access to water, so it had to pipe in its water from
the surrounding Lycus Valley. There were two other cities in
the Lycus Valley. One was called Hierapolis, the other Colossae. In Hierapolis there were steaming hot waters renowned
for their healing properties. In Colossae there was cold, pure

water, fresh and renewing to the taste. In Laodicea the water arrived lukewarm and initially, before settling, useless for anything apart from an emetic—a medicinal procedure to make someone vomit.

They think they are wealthy, but Jesus is pointing out their vulnerability. They had wealth—who could deny it? They also had tepid, stagnant, putrid water. When Jesus says in verse 16, "I will spit you out of my mouth," that is a rather polite translation. He is saying "I am about to vomit you out of my mouth. You know that tepid, lukewarm, deposit-encrusted water that makes you vomit if you don't treat it right first? Well, that's exactly how you make me feel, church at Laodicea. How I wish you were either hot, like the bubbling, beautiful waters at Hierapolis, or cold, like the refreshing springs at Colossae. But instead, you just think you're so perfect, but really you make me sick."

It's the only time such an emotion is predicated of God in the Bible. He is not angry. He is not disappointed. He is disgusted. But there is grace; there is room for a change of heart, as we'll see.

They must realize that they have to buy from Jesus "gold refined by fire." They may have riches, but there is a kind of wealth they do not have and desperately need.

JESUS IS NECESSARY EVEN FOR THOSE WHO THINK THEY ARE BEAUTIFUL

Again, in verse 17, we see that they think they don't need anything, "not realizing that you are wretched, pitiable, poor, blind, and naked." Jesus counsels them—how gentle and friendly is that word—he counsels them to buy from him "white garments so that you may clothe yourself and the shame of your nakedness may not be seen."

Not only was Laodicea famous for its wealth in general; in particular it had an international trade in textiles. One garment became so widely known that at the much later Council of Chalcedon in AD 451, Laodicea was simply referred to by the name of the garment, the *trimata*. Yet, beautifully dressed as they were, the church in Laodicea was really naked. Nakedness in biblical phraseology is often associated with shamefulness. While in the garden of Eden, Adam and Eve were both naked and felt no shame. Since then nakedness evoked wretchedness. And being given clothes meant approval and blessing. So Pharaoh granted Joseph new clothes when he was advanced to his position of vice-regent over Egypt. And the prophet Isaiah walked naked for three years as a sign of the coming judgment upon Israel through Assyria.

They are to buy clothes from Jesus, not meaning that such blessing is not a free gift but rather once more revealing their superficial self-reliance. "Buy," that is, go to the market, the market town that they were so proud of being; they thought they were the great commercial buyers and sellers at a profit; yet it was they who needed to buy and to receive from Jesus.

It's as if Jesus is saying to a successful sports team, "You think you've got the competition completely sown up and you're going to win it yet again, but actually it's you who need to learn just how to pitch! You can't even get the thing over the plate; you can't even kick the ball, let alone score a goal."

They were this great textile center—and it was they who had to import clothes from Jesus!

Jesus Is Necessary Even for Those Who Think They Are Healthy

In verse 17 they don't think they need anything; they just don't see it. But in verse 18, we're told that this is because they need to buy from Jesus "salve to anoint your eyes, so that you may see."

Once more the irony is thick. Laodicea was a medical center with a specialization in ophthalmology. And it was they who needed to import "salve" to put on their eyes? It's possible, actually, that a certain reputed ancient formula for improving eye problems, called "Phrygian powder" was made locally. Certainly, the medical school at Laodicea was founded by a person who had been mentored by a specialist in this area. They have the eyesight thing all sorted, so they believe, but Jesus tells them to buy some from him because they are not seeing straight, or even seeing at all. "You are blind," and you need some salve so that you can see!

What was going on? How was it that they seemed so respectable, organized, wealthy, well clothed, balanced, and yet were really, pitiful, poor, naked, and wretched? They would not have realized it. This of all the letters must have come as a shock. They were doing just fine, they thought. They *were* neither cold nor hot; they were avoiding those dangerous extremes. They arrived at verse 15 when the letter was first read out and everyone would have been nodding and saying,

"Yes, quite so. We are neither hot nor cold, thank goodness, praise the Lord," and suddenly Jesus points out the issue. Yes, neither cold nor hot—you're lukewarm like that tepid water that makes you throw up.

But what was the root of the problem?

There are hints here, if we look carefully. Note in verse 14 how Jesus introduces himself: "The words" is the standard introduction that we saw earlier. Only Pergamum answered with also holding on to the word: "The words of the Amen, the faithful and true witness, the beginning of God's creation." The Amen is Hebrew, of which the phrase "faithful and true witness" is an expansion for the non-Hebrew speakers in the congregation. God is the God of truth; he is *the truth*, the God of Amen, as John is prob-

> Jesus is *The Amen*, he is God, and he is absolutely necessary for all spiritual prosperity, wealth, true wealth, clothing, true clothing, seeing, true seeing.

ably picking up the divine epithet in Isaiah 65:16. He is the real and true God; this is Jesus. "The Amen, the faithful and true witness" and, note, "the beginning of God's creation." He is the "beginning" of creation, not the first thing created, but the active principle of creation, the source, the originator, the preeminent "uncreated principle...of creation" as one scholar puts it.[6]

This sounds very much like Colossians 1:15 and following, where Jesus is exalted in similar terms as the ruler of all, the uncreated principle of creation, the God, the "I AM," the beginning:

> He is the image of the invisible God, the firstborn of all creation. For by him all things were created, in heaven and on earth, visible and invisible, whether thrones or dominions or rulers or authorities—all things were created through him and for him. And he is before all things, and in him all things hold together. And he is the head of the body, the church. He is the beginning, the firstborn from the dead, that in everything he might be preeminent. For in him all the fullness of God was pleased to dwell, and through him to reconcile to himself all things, whether on earth or in heaven, making peace by the blood of his cross. (Colossians 1:15-20)

The Colossians, you see, were just down the road from Laodicea, fewer than ten miles or so. They were in constant communication; it's possible that their pastor at the time was drawn from the congregation in Colossae. At any rate, they were close; they knew each other well, and it's likely that the same doctrinal issues that troubled the Colossians were impinging on the Laodiceans, if in somewhat of a different form. In Colossae, there was probably a troubling tendency to give way to a syncretized form of Christianity, whereby Jesus became just one among many of the angelical powers of God mediating creation. Instead, Jesus is powerfully proclaimed by Paul as God himself, the ruler of creation.

Here, too, in Laodicea, less doctrinal, more practical, the Laodiceans were marginalizing Jesus. But Jesus is *The Amen,* he is God, and he is absolutely necessary for all spiritual prosperity, wealth, true wealth, clothing, true clothing, seeing, true seeing.

The Laodicean material prosperity combined with a hearsay of aberrant teaching down the road to give the church at Laodicea a feeling, a nice lukewarm feeling, that they could do it without Jesus. "God" was quite enough. But Jesus is the Amen, and it is with *him personally* that they must do business; they must "buy" gold, clothes, and eye salve.

For religion without Jesus is useless. It's just an emetic.

Now we can hear with clarity those famous words of Jesus captured in Holman Hunt's painting *The Light of the World*. "Behold," Jesus says, "I stand at the door and knock. If anyone hears my voice and opens the door, I will come in to him and eat with him, and he with me."

This too is laced in local significance. So rich were the Laodiceans that after the recent earthquake it was their boast that they alone of all the cities of Asia had rebuilt their city without imperial aid. Just recently they had relaid a magnificent triple gate to the city. Now they could keep out whom they would. With the Roman abuse of the ancient hospitality practice by billeting officials at great expense to the ruin of the wealthier inhabitants sometimes, that gate was good news for the Laodiceans. Jesus, though, is standing at it. He is not forcing his entry. He is knocking. He is not only knocking; he is calling, "If anyone hears my voice." And the meal of hospitality for which he is seeking entry is a meal of friendship: "I will come in to him and eat with him, *and he with me."*

What is remarkable about these words is that they are

written to a church, to Christians. "Behold I stand at the door and knock. If anyone hears my voice and opens the door, I will come in to him and eat with him, and he with me."

Jesus Is Necessary for All of Us

What are we doing to keep Jesus at arm's length? Are we frightened he will change us? Are we scared he will abuse our vulnerability? Will you open the door of your heart to Jesus today, for the first time, once more? What will happen when you do? "I will come in." Jesus has promised; it will be so. "I will come in to him and eat with him, and he with me." What will happen will be a reestablished friendship, symbolized by the friendship meal, between you and the Amen, the Lord Jesus Christ.

"We don't need Jesus as our friend," the voice says! "We have church! We have money! We have need of nothing!"

Without him you have nothing. For only with him, and being friends with him—not in a trite, small-minded, petty sense, but in the glory of intimacy with the Amen, the Lord himself—will you sit on the throne of destiny, of rulership in the age to come, in the life to come after death.

"He who has an ear, let him hear what the Spirit says to the churches." Open the door to Jesus today. Who knows? Maybe even you need a friend in heaven.

Notes

Monday: A Day for Hope

1. J. R. R. Tolkien, *The Fellowship of the Ring* (New York: Random House, 2012), 82.

2. Winston Churchill, "We Shall Fight on the Beaches," The Churchill Centre, accessed September 14, 2016, www.winstonchurchill.org /resources/speeches/1940-the-finest-hour/128-we-shall-fight-on -the-beaches.

3. Peter Brown, *Augustine of Hippo: A Biography* (Berkeley: University of California Press, 2000), 100–101.

Tuesday: A Day for Life

1. Oliver O'Donovan, *Ways of Judgment* (Grand Rapids: Eerdmans, 2008), 128.

Thursday: A Day for Freedom

1. Fyodor Dostoyevsky, *Brothers Karámazov*, trans. David Magarshack (New York: Penguin, 1987), 691.

2. Elie Wiesel, *Night* (New York: Hill and Wang, 2006), 33.

3. M. G. Archibald, "Come and Serve the Master," is song 19 in a chorus book produced by the Children's Special Service Mission in London in the early twentieth century.

4. Os Guinness, *Fool's Talk* (Downer's Grove, IL: InterVarsity, 2015), 83.

5. Richard Ellmann, *Oscar Wilde* (New York: Random House, 1984), 575.

Friday: A Day for Humility

1. C. S. Lewis, *Mere Christianity* (New York: HarperCollins, 1952), 112.

2. Roy F. Baumeister, Jennifer D. Campbell, Joachim I. Krueger, and Kathleen D. Vohs, "Does High Self-Esteem Cause Better Performance, Interpersonal Success, Happiness, or Healthier Lifestyles?" in *Psychological Science in the Public Interest*, vol. 4, no. 1 (May 2003): 1–44.

3. Jean M. Twenge, *Generation Me* (New York: Atria, 2006).

4. Charles Wesley, "Love Divine, All Loves Excelling," in *The United Methodist Hymnal* (Nashville: The United Methodist Publishing House, 1989), 384.

5. Ibid.

6. Herodotus, *Histories*, in *Herodotus, with an English Translation by A. D. Godley*, 4 vols. (Cambridge, MA: Harvard University Press, 1920), bk. 1, chap. 84.

7. Justin Martyr, "Dialogue with Trypho," in *Ante-Nicene Fathers: Translations of the Writings of the Fathers down to A.D. 325*, ed. Alexander Roberts and James Donaldson (Buffalo, NY: Christian Literature Publishing Company, 1885), 1:242–43.

Sunday: A Day for Glory

1. Robert D. Abrahams, "The Night They Burned Shanghai," *The Saturday Evening Post*, vol. 211, issue 39 (March 25, 1939): 70.

2. Frances Angermayer, "Conversion." Written in June 1943 and appeared in numerous publications.

3. Vladimir Nabokov, *Speak, Memory*, rev. ed. (New York: G. P. Putnam's Sons, 1966).

4. Jean Henri Merle d'Aubigné, *History of the Reformation of the 16th Century*, vol. 4, bk. 14 (1871), 395.

5. William Ramsay, *The Historical Geography of Asia Minor* (London, 1890), 4:49.

6. G. Abbott-Smith, *A Manual Greek Lexicon of the New Testament* (New York: Charles Scribner's Sons, 1922), 62.